FROM
Rock Bottom
TO
Mountaintop

This book is designed to help you get a hold on your feelings—to let you handle them instead of them handling you. You can read it by yourself or with the help of a group. A leader's guide, with visual aids (SonPower Multiuse Transparency Masters) is available from your local Christian bookstore or from the publisher.

FROM
Rock Bottom
TO
Mountaintop

Making sense out of your ups and downs

Bill Stearns

VICTOR BOOKS

a division of SP Publications, Inc.

WHEATON, ILLINOIS 60187

Offices also in Fullerton, California • Whitby, Ontario, Canada • Amersham-on-the-Hill, Bucks, England

Second printing, 1980

All Bible quotations, unless otherwise indicated, are from the *New American Standard Bible*, © 1960, 1962, 1963, 1968, 1971, 1972, 1973, 1975, The Lockman Foundation. Other quotations are from the *New International Version* (NIV), © 1978, The New York International Bible Society, and from the King James Version.

Library of Congress Catalog Card Number: 79-65040
ISBN: 0-88207-580-2

© 1979, SP Publications, Inc. All rights reserved
Printed in the United States of America

VICTOR BOOKS
A division of SP Publications, Inc.
P.O. Box 1825 ● Wheaton, Ill. 60187

To Janey

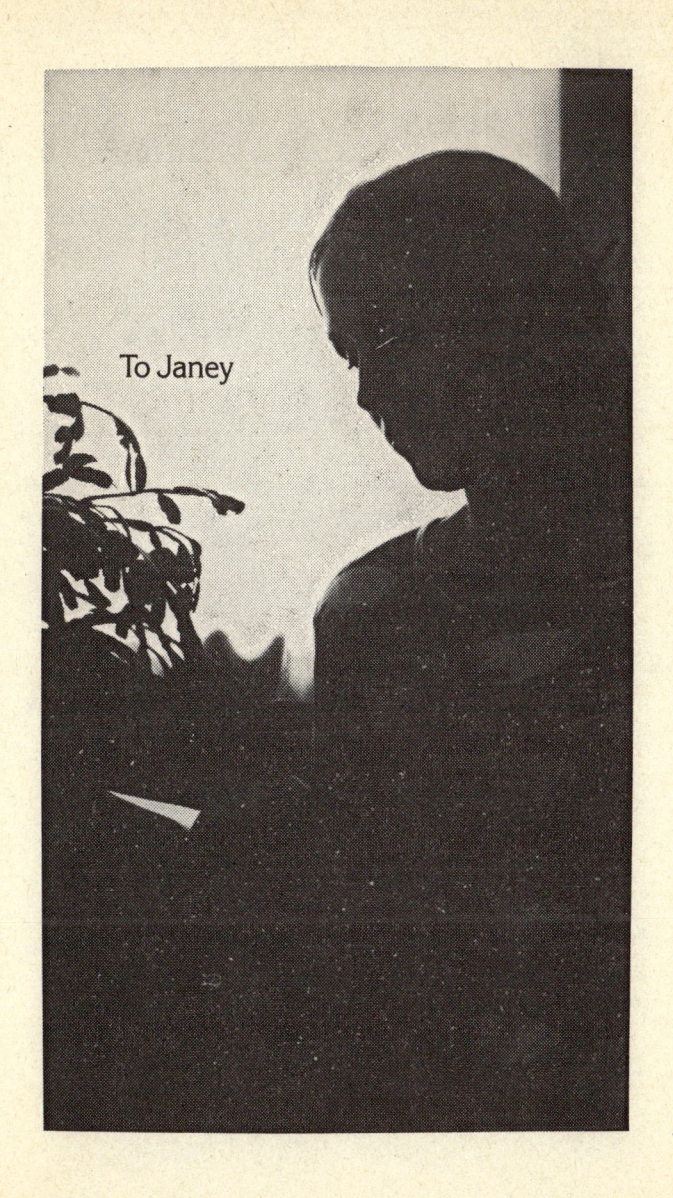

Contents

Author's Note 8

1 *Feelings*
  How Deep Is Your Valley,
  How High Is Your Hill? 11

2 *Love*
  Sparks and Flames 31

3 *Loneliness*
  Stuck between the Good Times 51

4 *Guilt*
  The Squeeze You Can't Avoid 81

5 *Anger*
  Don't Sizzle, Don't Explode 107

6 *Depression*
  Don't Bug Me Today 129

7 *Joy*
  Catch Those Fantastic Feelings 145

Author's Note

Listen, right off the bat I'll hit you with what this book *isn't:*

It's not a technical treatise on emotional psychology. So don't look for 14-syllable terminology or scholarly psychological theory. Expect instead that it'll just be plain old me talking to plain old you about God's views on feelings.

Second, the book isn't a do-it-yourself emotional surgery kit. We're not going to plunge into therapeutic treatments for severe emotional disorders. If that's the kind of help you need, grab a Christian counselor.

And finally, let's not kid each other that we're going to cover everything about feelings. We won't even touch all kinds of feelings. We won't get into physical feelings such as hunger or sunburn. And there's a lot more that can be said about even the feelings we *will* study. Because feelings are elusive, changing. They skitter around inside us like bubbles in 7-UP. You've probably felt feelings that don't even have names. So don't panic—this won't be an exhaustive study.

This book *is* a simple look at a few feelings as God-given signals to growth. So feel free to relax and enjoy our study together. Go ahead. Feel free!

—Bill

Feelings

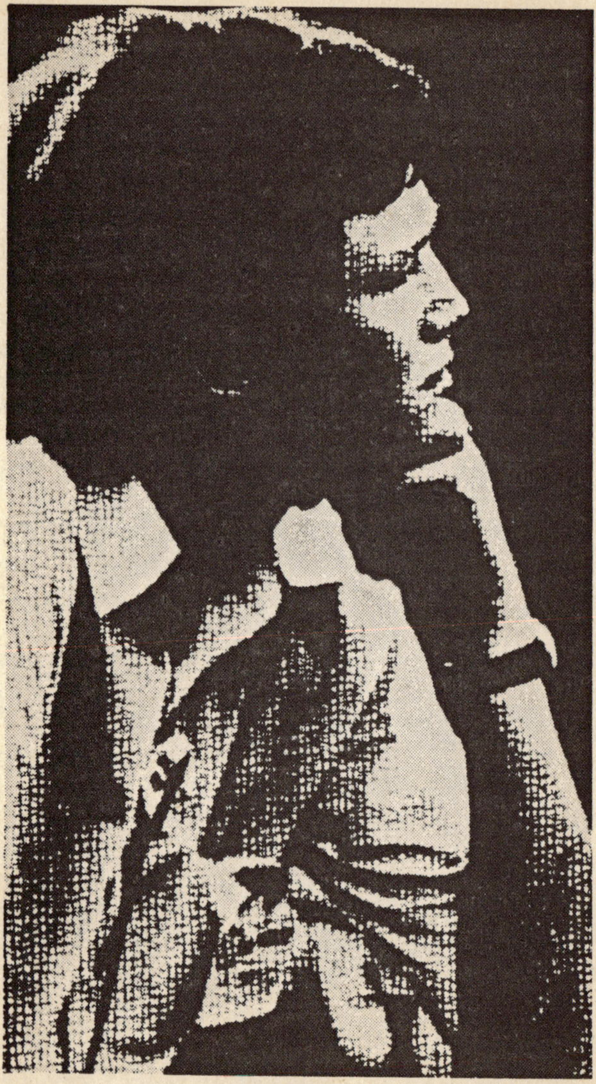

1
How Deep Is Your Valley, How High Is Your Hill?

Midnight fog thickened the darkness as he felt his way through the trees. The mist soaked his clothes, dripped across his face. He could see nothing in the blackness.

He scraped against a boulder and stopped, hugging cold granite as he breathed in rhythm to his heartbeat. How long now before they would find him? Before they'd break through the men who followed him as rear guards? "Watch for me," he'd simply said; and the men nodded, weary, but loyal for now.

He knew the authorities had been informed of his destination. He visualized the adrenaline-powered mob back in the town—the vigilantes and crack troops igniting each other's anger and the clatter of weapons.

He'd watched mobs before. Like dogs sniffing

blood, the townsfolk snarled when a captured woman had been led in. Their sneers were gleeful, evil. The authorities had played her before the crowd, dangling her near the mob as they dragged her away. He knew then what was in them: the lust for pain in someone else, as their eyes looked on her helplessness, while they craved the excitement of splattering blood. The women had spit on her; the men had ripped at her clothes.

Violence. He also knew what they'd do to him. Any time now.

His terror led to nausea. He choked in the blackness. He'd been up since dawn, feeling a frantic need to touch his friends one last time before he was taken. "We'll stand with you," they had promised. But he sensed the agony in their eyes. "You know the government tortures dissidents. We've got families." Some had even come with him. Loyal men. But were they still following him?

"Hey!" he whispered back down the path. Then he shouted, "Hey!" No one answered from the darkness. He was alone.

The damp of the night crowded in around him, and he stumbled on, drizzle and boulders and demons drenching his mind. The prayer came as a groan from his guts: "Father—God." He plodded on—eyes squeezing tears and mist—as if wading through a river of leeches that sucked for his life. He fell to his knees. "Father, if there's any way—" He clenched his fists and collapsed face forward in the mud. "Please—" The world swirled inside his head. He felt sick. "Any other way . . ." He

How Deep Is Your Valley / 13

struggled to rise. "But not My will. Not My will but Yours—"

And Jesus stood in Gethsemane to wait for His kiss.

Feelings are real. And strangely enough, they're designed to be felt. Even Jesus Christ—the perfect God-Man—feels wild feelings. He feels anger, joy, grief, amazement, pity, peace, and deep sorrow. He is "touched with the feelings of our infirmities" (Hebrews 4:15, KJV). In fact, He is so much the Model of how to handle feelings that the Bible says anyone not identified with Him will lose his sensitivity to real feelings! (Ephesians 4:17-19)

Feeling Feelings

It's good to be sensitive to feelings. It's all right to feel peace, happiness, joy, and compassion—mountaintop feelings. And hold onto your hats, it's even all right to experience envy, guilt, anger, loneliness, depression, sorrow, and fear—depending on how you handle those rock-bottom feelings!

What ain't so good is to *be handled* by feelings, to be pushed into a decision or action by a feeling. Have you ever walked into McDonald's when a McDonald-costumed person asks, "May I help you?" But you haven't had time to decide? You suddenly feel dumb—*I must be the slowest person in McDonald-land to pick out what I want!* You panic—*Oh, no! The McDonald-person is still waiting for me and there's 4.8 billion people behind me starving for a hamburger!*" And the feeling pushes you into blurting out, "Big Mac, order of fries, Coke, and McDonald-land cookies!" when you really just wanted a chocolate shake. Feelings can get to be pretty powerful, and they can push pretty hard: "I don't know what got into us," the boy mumbles. "We were just getting into each other physically, and then it felt like we couldn't stop." The kid slurs from the cell, "We just felt like doin' somethin' crazy, that's all. We didn't mean no harm to nobody."

So we can't let feelings handle us. Instead we need to handle feelings, enjoying the positive ones and dealing with the negative ones.

Positives. Feelings are responses to what we're doing, to what's happening to us, to what we're thinking. When we do or experience or think something positive, our responding mountaintop feelings of joy or peace or freedom or whatever tell us, "Hey, that's all right! Do it again!"

Ken Nichols always wore a helmet when he rode his motorcycle—except for that one morning. He was flying along as usual right in front of Leigh High School when he crashed. Dozens of his friends watched the whole thing. And I was asked as his youth pastor to say something at the funeral. I don't remember what I said as I stood before hundreds of crying, shocked high schoolers, but I remember clearly the incredible joy I sensed after Kenny's death.

Everybody's really upset, I told myself. *Maybe I'm weird. I'm not supposed to feel good about a*

How Deep Is Your Valley / 15

friend dying like this. But I did. I remember being very sad-faced throughout the funeral and burial, almost feeling guilty about the way I felt inside.

The next day, I ran a couple miles on the beach, thinking about Kenny's huge grin, his happy disposition, his growth as a Christian, his skill at mischief. I stopped, yelled "Yahoo!" and grinned at the sky. I knew—I'd known all along—that Ken was still grinning as grandly as ever, enjoying himself in ways I couldn't even understand. He was, on that day, perfectly Christlike. He beat me to it.

Without being disrespectful to his family or other friends, I found I could enjoy my understanding of Ken's death. The joy I felt reinforced the positive way I was thinking about the death of a Christian.

Feelings that result from positive experiences are

to be enjoyed. Go ahead—laugh when you're happy. Close your eyes, and relish feelings of peace. Recognize what caused the nice feeling and—if it's a true feeling—repeat it. Think those thoughts again; act that same way again; put yourself in those same circumstances. It's OK to enjoy good feelings!

Negatives. When you do something or think something or go through an experience that's negative, your resulting rock-bottom feelings signal a problem that needs to be corrected. Grief, anger, jealousy, loneliness, depression, guilt, fear, envy, and other painful emotions are actually God-given danger signs that say, "Something's wrong." The feelings tell you to go back and straighten out that act or thought and adjust yourself correctly to that experience. These feelings are no fun; they make you feel like you're right on the bottom. But they can be useful in your life if *you* handle them. They can be destructive if you let *them* handle you.

Candi lost all contact with her father when her folks divorced. When David came into her life she felt as if the void her father had left was almost filled. David was in college while Candi was still in high school. The romance flourished, till David dropped Candi and started dating her best friend.

Candi's rage was awesome. The jealousy she felt consumed her, pushed her into depression, drove her toward bitterness. She felt hurt, embarrassed, angry.

It took her nearly six months to decide that all these negative feelings were basically pointing to one thing: She thought she was lost without a man.

Her rough feelings were a signal of this attitude problem. She came to understand the positive biblical idea that with God, she was completely secure—with or without a father, boyfriend, or husband.

See how painful feelings work to point out problems? Another example: Sarah woke up feeling guilty. She didn't need to examine the feeling for long. Her guilt told her that acting in the sexually loose way she had the night before was not the way to live.

Use those negative experiences to motivate yourself toward correcting the problem. When you're sad, do something about it. When you feel guilty, admit and confess your guilt; then straighten out what you did wrong. If you feel grief, realize that it's pointing you toward filling your loss with new relationships. If you're lonely, admit it; then take action to fill your day with relationships. Listen to your "bad" feelings. (They're not really bad unless you handle them badly. They're just painful.) They'll tell you something's wrong.

False feelings. Now, hopefully, if you've been thinking through these ideas and aren't just skimming—Of course you wouldn't just skim through such lofty concepts. I mean, what kind of numbskull would get hold of a book and then not think about what it's saying? What are you, a jerk? A low-down, shameful cur?

Forgive me. What I was trying to do in that paragraph was make you feel guilty. To feel false guilt. Guilt that you don't really deserve. It probably didn't work, right? But here's a situation where false feelings did work:

Jonathan always felt that his dad had something against him, and when he was 13 he found out what it was. His dad got drunk one night and stumbled into the house to taunt Jonathan, saying, "You're illegitimate, you lousy kid. Figure it out—our marriage date was two months after you were born. You forced me into this stinkin' rat race—"

From that year on, Jon felt as if all the family's troubles were his fault. He would clam up if any mention were made of his birthday or his parents' anniversary. He shunned any close relationships for fear someone would find out. Even as a young man he was plagued with feelings of insecurity, bitterness, and guilt. Mostly guilt.

If Jonathan's guilt feelings were *true* feelings, they would reflect that it was his fault for being born illegitimately. But was his guilt *true* guilt? The accuracy of a feeling can be determined by how it measures up to the truth, God's Word.

Jonathan's guilt feelings say, "You were wrong to be born illegitimately," but God *nowhere* in His Word says that anyone is guilty for what his mother and father may have done. Which is true: the feeling or God? Jonathan was drowning in false, unnecessary, painful feelings.

Freddie Schwartz sniffs airplane glue and feels high and joyful. Is this good feeling a true one which tells him to do it till his nostrils seal shut?

Derek Dynamic feels *lousy* when he's apologizing to a friend. Does his lousy feeling mean he should never apologize? Nope. All these are false feelings.

God says it's not OK to have sex before marriage; so when the guy and the girl feel *good* about it, it's a false feeling. The feeling says, "Make it a habit," while God says, "Flee from sexual immorality" (1 Corinthians 6:18, NIV). On the other hand, God says it's OK to enjoy sex in marriage—but a clean-living couple may feel guilty because they think sex is evil. The false feeling says, "You're not supposed to enjoy sex," while God says that sex in marriage is honorable and pure (Hebrews 13:4).

God's Word strips the fluff away from false feelings. So, friends and neighbors, be aware and be wary of your feelings. If the feelings are true, enjoy them or correct the signaled problems. If they're false as revealed by the Bible, realize that their advice is false. Make sense?

Expressing Feelings

The wind has been rising since dawn. Already the crew has forgotton about drilling, and in my first week aboard rig #19—an offshore oil platform 137 miles out in the Gulf of Mexico—my stomach cringes at every wave. The water is black. It rolls in heavy humps to first smash underneath the platform, then blasts in spray across the deck. The saltwater slaps my face. The thick power of the sea, the wind pulling everything aboard toward the east into the water, reminds me that I'm clinging to a pinhead—a nuts-and-bolts tree house that's rooted hundreds of feet below the surging surface. I imagine hearing the clatter of a helicopter coming in through the mud gray clouds to take me home, but it's only the shudder of the platform at the shove of every wave. There'll be no chopper—gale winds are mounting, so evacuation by sea is the only way I'll get off this rig. And linking up with a ship in these heavy seas makes that operation almost as dangerous as remaining aboard. I'm ordered below, and as I pass the radio room I hear the word. *Hurricane*. I feel—

How would *you* feel? Insecure? Worried? Scared? Are you *wrong* to feel painful feelings? No. Are there wrong ways to *express* your feelings? Yes. Feelings themselves are really neither bad nor good; the wrong/right and spirituality/non-spirituality of feelings lie in how we express them. Feeling a feeling is one thing; showing that feeling—whether positive or negative—is another matter altogether. There are basically two extremes to consider in showing feelings.

Don't cry out loud. A couple days ago I was sprawled in my usual dignified fashion across a New Orleans library lawn, thinking about what I'd say to you in this chapter. About the time my brain was getting numb from thinking so much about nothing, a 10-year-old with a cigarette wedged between his teeth plopped down on a nearby bench and turned his transistor radio all the way up. The first song that came on had great music and dumb advice. It was mama telling her daughter not to cry out loud but to "keep it inside; learn how to hide your feelings."

Handling your feelings by keeping them all bottled up inside will make you weird. Or sick. Or maybe even dead. You see, feelings were designed to be expressed. If you don't express them in positive ways, they'll sneak out to be expressed in other ways. Put yourself back on that offshore oil platform. If you felt scared (as I did), you *could* force yourself to act nonchalant and happy. But somehow the feeling would come out—maybe in shaking hands, a twitching eyelid, a lump in your throat, nausea, a step toward an ulcer, or even eventual emotional fears that couldn't be explained.

Boys are often taught that it's "unmanly" to cry. (And men have more ulcers than women.) Jumping up and clicking your heels in delight is not considered "adult." Sorrow is awkward, embarrassing. Society often seems to say that we're all just machines, so forget feelings—they just make you weak, vulnerable. Don't show that you care about someone—you'll just get hurt. Don't let anybody know you're angry—you'll just look like a fool. Don't get an ecstatic lump in your throat about patriotism—technology has no room for sentiment. Don't show your fear, your insecurity—somebody will take advantage of you. Don't cry out loud.

Christian people sometimes follow this way of expressing emotions. They think that since the Bible mentions walking by faith, feelings aren't important at all. "Ignore your feelings" is the message. "Christians shouldn't feel tension" is a typical theorem of this group. So if you're embroiled in an inner battle, you still need to seem calm on the surface to be "spiritual." If you feel fearful, just pretend you don't. If you feel insecure, doubting—don't breathe a word of it; that's just your human side showing. If you feel like leaping in joy, please just whisper a sober "isn't the Lord truly wonderful?" Some Christians even believe that not experiencing feelings is spiritual!

But we *do* experience feelings, and hypocritically acting as if we don't only brings on all kinds of physical disorders, irritated personalities, emotional conflicts. Psychosomatic diseases—physical ailments caused by unexpressed emotional conflicts—represent a huge percentage of medical cases in our society.

Keeping it hidden away inside is not the way for anybody—Christian or not—to handle feelings. For your own sake, don't squelch your feelings, whether they're positive or not.

If it feels good, don't hold back. Remember how I was sprawled on the library lawn listening to the kid's radio? Well, right after that good song with bad advice, a disco number came on with the lines, "If it feels good, don't hold back; if it feels good, don't hold back; if it . . ." You can guess how the rest of it went. The song hints at an opposite, just-as-extreme way of handling feelings: Just let 'em all hang out. Do what you feel.

While squelching all your feelings rots you from the inside, letting them all fly rots your relationships. If you're on an oil rig in a hurricane, you'll be scared. If you express your fear by shrieking and sobbing and screaming to the other crew members, your actions will affect them. They'll become more frightened themselves—with the result that nobody can think straight.

Here's another "for instance": Let's say you're dining elegantly at the Shuffle Inn and a guy shuffles in with a face like a three-week-old pizza. With your mouth full you yell, "Uggh! I feel revolted by you! You're ugly! Look at this guy, folks! I feel like throwing up every time I look at him!" Now maybe you actually feel that way. But your don't-hold-back expression of how you feel just totally destroyed any relationship you might ever have with the guy or with any other Shuffle Inn regulars.

A person who practices uncontrolled expression of his feelings will soon be left to himself. The kid who can't control his temper is a good example. He won't have many good friends. Or a lady who constantly moans and complains because of some sorrow she's feeling will eventually be avoided by others. Yelling "yahoo!" at a funeral because I sense the joy of Christian death isn't exactly smart. Letting it all out isn't the way to express feelings.

The Balance

There's a balance between the extremes of locking it all inside and letting it all out. The balance is a *controlled expression* of feeling.

How do you find that balance? By following a general pattern of acknowledging, examining, and *then* acting on your feelings. Stick with me, and let's think this three-step process through.

Acknowledge. Get in touch with your feelings. Most of us learn to disguise our feelings as we get older. So sometimes it's tough to retrace what we're really feeling. Recognizing your feelings may take some practice. Do you have feelings? Yes—even if you're not sensitive to them, even if you don't usually express them. What are those feelings? Just to give yourself an idea of the feelings you run through in a day, try recording them. Pick a good, active day; and jot down on a card what you're feeling about every half hour. Right, the first feeling you'd probably jot down would be "dumb"! Double-check yourself as you're writing down the feeling by asking, "Is this *really* what I feel?" For instance, maybe you'd jot down "happy" at 11:30 A.M., only to double-check yourself and find you're *really* feeling "free from pressure"—it's lunchtime! List the physical sensations as well as your emotions; you may see tie-ins between the two such as a 4:30 P.M. listing: "hungry" (physical sensation) and "impatient" (emotion).

Go ahead, do it. Feel stupid—it'll keep you humble. If anybody asks why you're writing on the card, just tell them you're doing research on "Life and How I Achieved It"; then jot down "embarrassed." Admit your feelings.

Examine. Figure out if your feelings are reflecting positive or negative actions or thoughts. Your examination of the feeling will reveal whether you need to practice your behavior or correct it. (Incidentally, if you feel guilty about examining yourself, you're feeling a false guilt! Study Romans 12:3; 1 Corinthians 11:28; and 2 Corinthians 13:5. You'll find that the popular religious maxim of "Don't ever think about yourself" *should* be, "Don't dwell on your *old* self, your old sinful nature self." We're *commanded* to examine ourselves.)

Examine your feelings in light of what God says in His Word. If the feelings reflect positive behavior according to God's Word, then they're there to reinforce your behavior. If your behavior was negative according to God's Word, the resulting feelings point out problems. They're signalling that you need to correct what you do, the way you think, or your adjustment to a situation.

Act. This is the *expression* part of handling your feelings. Once you've used your thinking cap in acknowledging and examining a feeling (a process which may take a couple hours or, for an emotionally mature person, a split second), *do* something about what you feel. The *doing* will automatically be a controlled expression of your acknowledged and examined feeling.

Talk about your feeling. To the Lord. To other people. To yourself. If you can't talk, write it out. Here's a written expression of how one girl felt when her father abandoned the family:

dear Father
I remember
you were my world
and
our big backyard
where we played chase and hide-and-seek

till Mother called us down
from football games and snow fights
my red bicycle with training wheels
and you running along beside me
more afraid than I
   I would remember with relief
my tearful good-byes
when you finally came home
I remember everything
especially
when you left
and never came home again
Mother
didn't even cry
I had to hide in my room
   and wait by the window
that fogged in my breath
you told her
soon I'd forget
after all
I was just a child

—Susan Munden

Action is a form of expression. Once you've enjoyed or endured a feeling, get your act together to either reinforce positive behavior or correct negative behavior. It doesn't take a great brain to figure out that if a session of real prayer brought you a feeling of peace, keep praying. If getting blasted on a half-gallon of Jim Beam left you guilty and ashamed, don't do it again.

Sometimes the action you need to take isn't outward. Maybe the wild anger you feel every time you lose at Ping-Pong is telling you to readjust your ego, not necessarily to quit playing Ping-Pong. Maybe the envy you feel toward a friend is pointing out a need to shift your values, to make an inward change—not to avoid the friend.

The End Is Coming

I could go on and on, giving illustrations about feelings. But let's quickly sum up what we've dealt with so far; then we can get down to the nitty-gritties of specific feelings.

- A feeling may be a God-given response.
- Feelings point out positive acts and thoughts for reinforcement and negative acts and thoughts for correction.
- Squelching a feeling can damage a person; letting it all out can damage relationships.
- The balanced, controlled expression of a feeling comes by acknowledging it, examining it for what it's pointing out, and then acting to reinforce or correct what caused it.

So feel free to feel feelings. And learn how to express them well. I'll be praying for you, so study hard as you think through specific feelings in the following chapters—from rock bottom to mountaintop!

Love

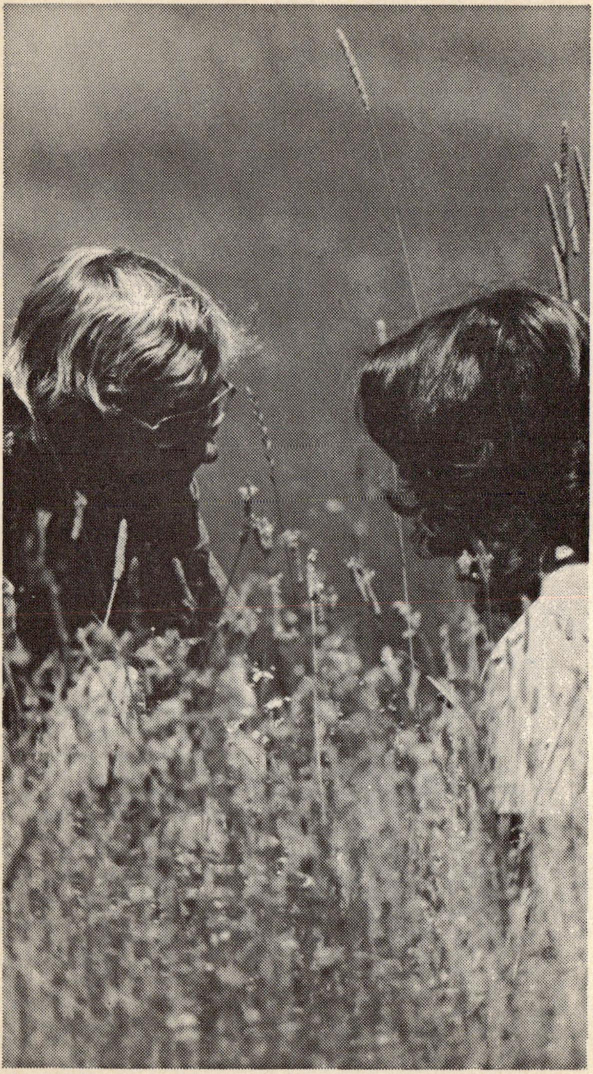

2
Sparks and Flames

He wasn't watching the play as he slid his elbow slightly into the soft arm of his date sitting beside him.

She kept staring at the stage. Maybe she didn't feel the elbow, he thought. But he did notice her sandaled foot resting against his shin.

The boy suddenly yawned and stretched his right arm behind her back, planting it across the top of her chair as his huge yawn subsided like a balloon with the air escaping.

"Bored?" she whispered. The real question was: Should she ignore the arm? Or should she respond with a twitch against his shin?

"Nope." The boy sat awkwardly. The back of her chair was higher than he'd planned; and now his arm was tingling, falling asleep. He watched the play again, wondering how the arguing actors were so easily led into passionate embraces when he couldn't even pull off his pre-date fantasies of snuggling amidst the popcorn.

The girl knew what he was thinking—and she felt sorry for him. She desperately wanted him to enjoy the drama. Was he really bored? Should she say something? But she certainly wouldn't want to appear like his mother. Finally she reached over and patted his knee twice. Her heart thumped in her throat as she left her sweating fingers on his kneecap.

He wondered immediately if his knee felt bony. He flexed his leg till he felt a cramp. The play droned on for another four minutes while he waited for his palm to stop perspiring enough to squeeze his hand into hers, which was still perched stiffly on his knee. Should he risk pulling his right arm—now dead asleep, unfeeling—from the top of her chair? Would his right hand be less sweaty than his left? Suddenly he flopped his left hand on top of hers, and he tilted even more in the seat. He croaked, "I love you."

The arm of the seat pressed into her side as she leaned to make room for him. "What?" she whispered.

The curtain dropped and the crowd began to applaud as he tried again. "I love you." His voice cracked.

The applause became a standing ovation, and the couple painfully unfolded to stand as the lights came up. "Quite a production!" she yelled at him over the noise of clapping.

"Yeah, I know what you mean," the boy shouted back. He smiled a little. "Some drama."

Two Fools Together

Love is good stuff. But not the dumb games or wild ecstasy most people think of as love. "Ecstasy" in Greek literally means only "deranged." I mean real love is good stuff. And love is something *you* can have—even if you consider yourself The World's Most Unlikely to Be Loved.

I've got a friend who says, "Life is just one fool thing after another, and love is just two fool things after each other." Clever? But there really aren't many more intelligent definitions of love around.

If there were a *perfect* definition of love, it would make sense that the details come from the Inventor of the thing. The Bible states simply that "God is love" (1 John 4:8), so obviously God is the One to tell us just exactly what love is:

• "The commandments, 'Do not commit adultery,' 'Do not murder,' 'Do not steal,' 'Do not covet,' and whatever other commandment there may be, are summed up in this one rule: 'Love your neighbor as yourself.' Love does no harm to its neighbor. Therefore love is the fulfillment of the Law" (Romans 13:9-10, NIV).

• "The entire Law is summed up in a single command: 'Love your neighbor as yourself' " (Galatians 5:14, NIV).

• "For this is the love of God, that we keep His commandments" (1 John 5:3).

• "And this is love: that we walk in obedience to His commands" (2 John 6, NIV).

Did you catch those verses? This is what love is:

34 / From Rock Bottom to Mountaintop

"that we walk in obedience to His commands"! God says that if we would do what He says in every area of our lives, if we follow His commands, we will be loving. Love is the accomplishing of God's commandments. Let's think this through a bit.

Three Relationships

There are three types of relationships you can enjoy in life: your relationship to God, to others, and to yourself. God's commandments in Scripture fall into three categories: commands regarding God, other people, and the self.

God knows how to reach the ultimate in relationships, and He tells us in the Bible how it's all done—the do's and don'ts of real love.

Love involves a choice between treating someone in accordance with God's commands or doing it whatever way feels good. Love is action and attitude—it is doing and being. *Love is a pattern of living "in obedience to His commands"!* (2 John 6, NIV)

What has this got to do with our study of feelings? Just this: Contrary to very popular opinion, love is *not* just a feeling.

Romance and Stuff

Reginald stood first on one foot, then the other. The ground was hot where he was standing to register for two weeks of summer camp. Then he forgot the heat and forgot he was standing on just one foot when he saw—*her!* Suntanned, with her nose cracked from sunburn (that's OK, he thought; noses heal), in just the right jeans and T-shirt. Face just a little too sweet but sophisticated too. The camp romance, the letters to each other for the next year, the incredible feeling that he'd been looking for her all his 14 years of life—Reggie was in love!

If the scene makes you laugh in reading it as much as it did me, I think you caught the point.

Yes, Reginald is feeling some pitter-patter in his chest. Yes, she's the girl of his dreams. And yes, it just might all work out. But is Reggie in love? Is he involved in a pattern of fulfilling God's commands toward the girl? Nope. He is, however, completely washed away in feelings of romance, infatuation, attraction. He's "fallen in love." That's all fine. Feelings are nice. They're enjoyable. But they're not real love. The divine description of love in 1 Corinthians 13 points out the actions and attitudes that characterize love. Nothing is said about sweaty palms or heart throbbings. Because love isn't just a feeling.

I definitely love my little daughter, Carrie Bea. No question about it. How do I know it's real love and not just a feeling? (This may seem like a dumb parallel to a guy/girl love relationship, but hang in there.) Carrie is a blonde-haired, blue-eyed kid who is very loud. And at night, being very loud, she regularly snaps me out of a deep 2 A.M. sleep with a screaming commentary on her nightmares from her room upstairs. I leap off the end of the bed into my wife's quilting frame, smack into the closed door which I thought was open because Carrie could be heard so clearly, and finally stumble upstairs to her bedroom. I gasp at the smell of her recently wet bed coming out of the darkness; and as I grope around on the bed trying to find her, I feel the kid-style drool and her runny nose. Finally I get a whiff of her eight-hour-old pizza breath. (Why didn't my wife remember to see that Carrie brushed her teeth before bed?)

Suddenly I remember I love her. My eyes mist over, I feel an overwhelming surge of pitter-patter in my chest, I smile, I feel warm and gushy all over. Right? Wrong. I've barely got my eyes open, I don't feel good, and the only thing that feels warm and gushy is the wet bed. I don't *feel* much, but I *know* that I love little Carrie Bea. Hugging away her nightmare is more important than my sleep. I don't care in the least what her appearance is right now. She is definitely not attractive at the moment. But I know I love her because my relationship with her is characterized by a pattern of—you guessed it—fulfilling God's commands toward her in both action and attitude.

Feelings and Attraction

Infatuation, if misunderstood, can be dangerous—you can romantically "love" anyone. You can "have feelings of love," "fall in love," be strongly attracted to anybody—even the wrong person for you! You can feel wildly attracted to someone, only to discover after you got to know the person that you really don't like him or her at all.

Carol always had Joe Grant's arm draped around her. All she could talk about was Joe this, Joe that. And Joe was bad—the first sophomore to grow enough hair on his chest to wear his shirts halfway unbuttoned. He was a dedicated macho-type who thrived on the ego-trip of Carol's worship. The two of them could hardly wait to graduate from high school so they could get married.

It was pretty obvious to everybody who knew them that Carol was completely starry-eyed about Joe. But he regularly messed around with other girls, ignored Carol for days at a time, and had a habit of making fun of her every chance he got. But sure enough, a few months after graduation, it was wedding bells. And within the year it was divorce court. Though I haven't had the chance to talk to Carol about the whole thing, it was obvious in their relationship that there was very little real love between the two of them. But they both had enjoyed all kinds of romantic feelings.

Anna was a Christian. Her boyfriend wasn't. She manipulated him into "counseling" sessions where her goal was to sic the minister on the guy—she had to get him saved before things got too serious because she *knew* the Bible gives a principle against a believer marrying an unbeliever (2 Corinthians 6:14). "I know it's dangerous getting more and more serious with him—but if God wanted us to break up,

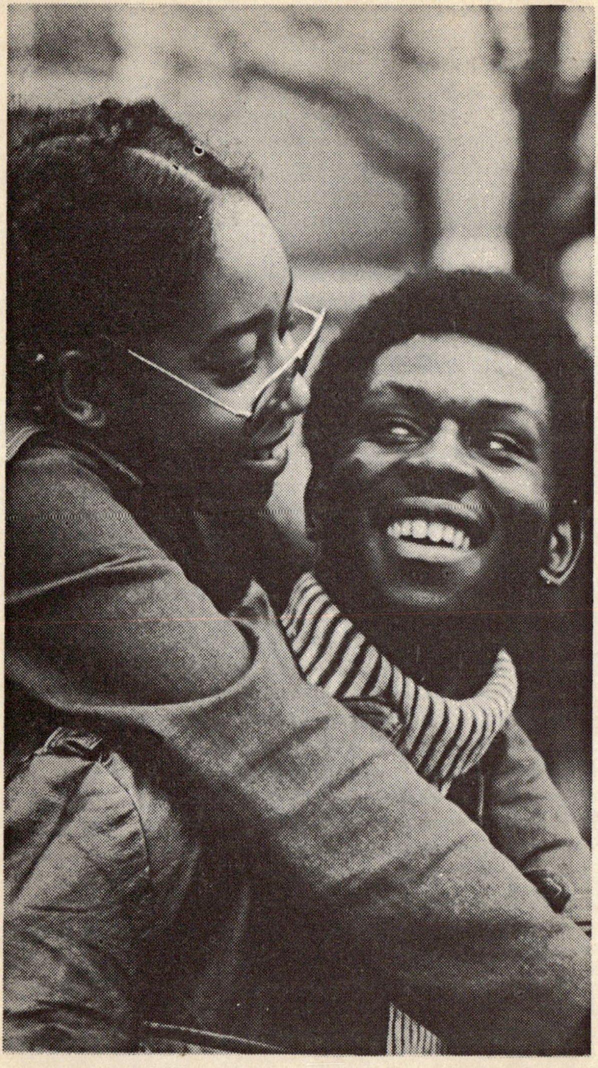

why is our love so strong? We can't deny what we feel!"

Yes you can. You can deny what you *feel* and sometimes you must. Feelings can mislead you. Think about it. A person can feel ecstatic about someone, jump into a sexual relationship, then feel nothing but disgust. A person who's fooled into thinking that love is a big warm feeling can marry because of those wild feelings; then when the feelings fade (gradually, temporarily, or even permanently), the thought comes: "Oh, oh. Love is gone. I must've married the wrong one!" Or a person who confuses racy romantic feelings with real love might marry, then years later find that she or he is wildly attracted to someone else. The thought, *He makes me feel those old feelings again!* is the basis for more sappy soap operas than you could count.

Just because you're romantically attracted to someone doesn't mean you're really in love. It doesn't mean that your current friend is The One. Your feelings can be wrong. There's a really stupid myth bouncing around that says you'll only "fall in love" with the one you're supposed to marry. That's crazy. You can have racy feelings or "fall in love" or be attracted to or be infatuated with or become romantically involved with almost anybody!

Romance VS Real Love Relationships

A lot of boyfriend/girlfriend relationships depend pretty much on feelings. And that's OK for a while.

40 / From Rock Bottom to Mountaintop

The couple keeps seeing each other because the two *feel* so fantastic whenever they're together. It feels good. And it is good. But real love—the lifestyle that treats someone in accordance with God's commands in both action and attitude—needs to take root and start growing to carry the couple through times when the two *aren't* feeling so fantastic. When they've had a huge argument. When they're depressed or discouraged. When one of them has failed miserably.

Feelings can come and go; but real love—Jesus-style—never fails. It literally never quits (1 Corinthians 13:8). If a relationship is built on romantic love, when the rough feelings of life inevitably crowd out the warm gushy feelings of infatuation, the partners often *feel* their relationship has fizzled. They think they now need to find someone else who can make them "feel love" again. See how dangerous a misunderstanding of love can be?

I also hate to say this one: A fulfilling marriage does not necessarily depend on romantic love. You know all those horrible old Eastern-hemisphere stories about "arranged marriages" where the bride and groom hardly know each other or don't even see each other till the wedding ceremony? Uncle Chou bartered a few pig ears and bolts of velvet for the bride, and the elders of the families arranged a very organized marriage. Sounds awful, right?

Well, I'm glad my marriage wasn't plotted on a blueprint for me or didn't depend on a fat pig; but the ancients weren't so far off in these customs. They knew that romance isn't necessarily the key to a successful and fulfilling marriage. Romance is definitely nice, but not really necessary. Real love can flourish even when two plain, non-attractive slobs maybe never really know feelings of romance/infatuation/attraction toward each other. They can love each other more deeply than the most chic jet set couple who seems to have all the qualities of being "lovable."

To Love or Not to Love

"¡Sí, Se Puede!" I ran across that message on a bumper sticker in Phoenix a few years ago. It might be a good motto for believers. It means "Yes, you can!" You can decide to love or not to love because God says that anyone can love. It simply (simply?) takes an effort of your will. You can enjoy real love at a depth that would make the Romeo-and-Juliet story look like kid stuff. Love isn't something that suddenly bonks you on the head, though feelings *will* do that. Romantic love/infatuation will hit you with feelings of attraction whether you want them or not. But real love is not "something out there," a little cupid with an arrow. God gives us a choice as to whether we want to enjoy real love or not. How do I know that?

Christ said, "By this all men will know that you are My disciples, if you have love for one another" (John 13:35). Notice the "if." People will know we belong to Christ *if* we're loving each other. It's possible not to be loving. God wouldn't give us a com-

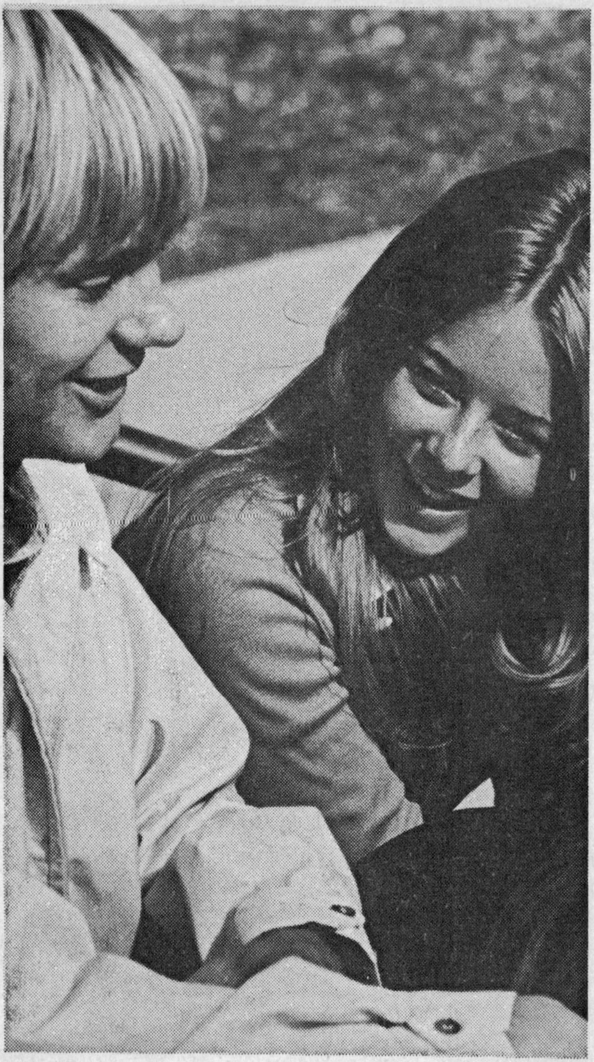

mand if we didn't have a choice about obeying it. We have a choice: to love or not to love.

Look at it this way: God doesn't have to write a huge commandment in the Bible saying, "Breathe!" because we automatically do it. We have no choice if we're alive other than to breathe. But God did say, "Don't murder!" Since He had to give it as a command, this tells us that we have a choice either to murder or not to murder. But the whole point is that since we have a choice, we can *decide* to love.

Jesus even says it's possible to love your enemy! (Matthew 5:44) Why? Because you should feel warm, gushy feelings for someone who's out to slit your throat? No, you can love your enemy regardless of what he does because you *decide* as a matter of your will to fulfill God's commands toward him in action and attitude. Love is not a feeling you wait for. Real love involves a choice.

Anyone Can Love!

And if choosing whom to love isn't good news, I don't know what is! If you're a young woman who knows that you'll never quite fit into the "sleeping beauty" role of romance, or if you're a guy who knows that you don't have massive shoulders and a deep voice and all the other trappings of the typical "man of her dreams"—cheer up! You can enjoy the most fantastic love relationship the world has ever known! Really. Since loving is something you *decide* to do and isn't something a fairy godmother sprinkles on a few select beauty queens and princes, *you* can decide to be loving. You can decide to fulfill toward another person the actions and attitudes of God's commandments, outlined in the Bible.

God's idea of stepping into a love relationship isn't to become more and more attractive, to make yourself lovable. Millions of dollars worth of advertising to the contrary, you can love and be loved even if you have zits. The path to a real love relationship isn't through making yourself lovable—by wearing the right perfume, by driving the right car, by using the right breath mint or toothpaste, by buying the right clothes. The whole commercial system of our society's economy seems often to be one big statement: In order to be the couple who runs bouncing in slow motion toward each other's arms in the meadow, you only have to wear a certain deodorant and use a certain cream rinse on your curly locks. The message of commercial media is: Be glamorous or have machismo—be lovable!

But God, the Expert on love, says, *be loving.* No one may be bowled over by you; no one may *ever* be ecstatically infatuated with you; you may never be wildly attractive to anyone. But you can enjoy the richest love relationship possible by following God's advice:

"All men will know you are My disciples if you love one another" (John 13:35, NIV).

"This is My commandment, that you love one another" (John 15:12).

"Let all that you do be done in love" (1 Corinthians 16:14).

"You yourselves are taught by God to love one another" (1 Thessalonians 4:9).

Anyone can get in on the good stuff of real love—not by selfishly concentrating on being lovable, but by allowing Christ to control actions and attitudes according to God's commandments.

Loving Takes Effort

If real loving comes through a decision process, it's going to be tough sometimes to practice it. The luxurious feelings of romantic love/infatuation just drift across your nerve endings effortlessly, automatically. It's easy to "fall in love." In fact it's so effortless that sometimes two people become strongly attracted to each other even when they don't *want* to be. But attraction isn't real love, remember. Real love takes effort. An effort of the will.

Love Is a Process

Romantic love usually hits you hardest at first; then the feelings fade with time as the novelty wears off. Feelings are like that: The first day you hold somebody's hand you feel good feelings; after ten years of hand-holding the feeling isn't quite such a big deal. But real love goes in just the opposite direction: It begins slowly, simply, then grows in depth and power. The decisions—acts of the will—to fulfill God's commands toward a person become more

```
Guy/girl Relationships
------ feelings of attraction/infatuation
——— real love
```

Intensity in a relationship

Length of time of a relationship

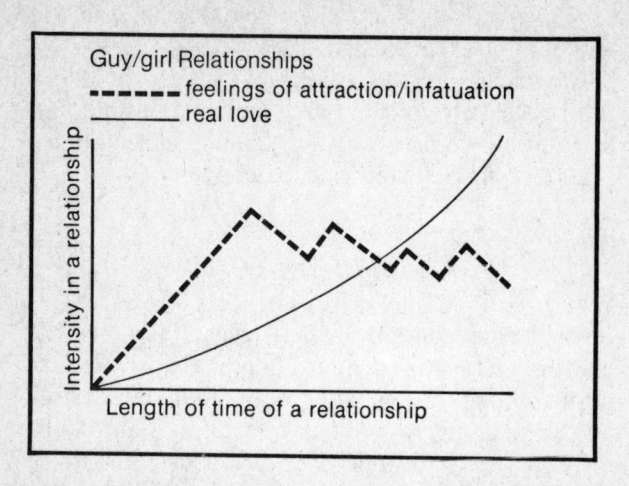

and more frequent with practice. As I learn how to put into practice more effectively the actions and attitudes God prescribes, my ability to love grows. It becomes a pattern, a process which develops in intensity during the relationship. Real love isn't a one-shot extravaganza—it's a long-term process.

In the beginning of a relationship, the initial feelings of romantic love/attraction will motivate me to fulfill God's commandments toward a person. Have you ever noticed how easy it is for a foul-mouthed clod of a guy to suddenly become a perfect gentleman when an attractive girl is present? The feelings of infatuation carry built-in motivation to treat the person properly. These feelings are good and are to be enjoyed. But eventually if and when the feelings fade, the will—the ability to make decisions—must take over in motivating a person to treat someone else according to God's commands. A person loves not just because he *feels* like it but because he's *decided* to love. Make sense?

And the desire to decide can develop. Real love isn't static; it grows deeper. Richer. Paul prays that "love may abound still more and more in real knowledge and all discernment" (Philippians 1:9). How does love grow? In real knowledge—knowing more of God's commands. And love is to grow in all discernment—knowing how in quiet sensitivity to apply and fulfill those commands in the life of the loved one. Love can abound!

And in Summary

Love is good stuff. It's a growing process. A deciding process. Any Christian can decide to fulfill toward another—even toward enemies—the actions and attitudes talked about in God's commandments. Any Christian can love—because real love is not a feeling. It's a pattern of deciding to treat a person the way God would treat him.

Loneliness

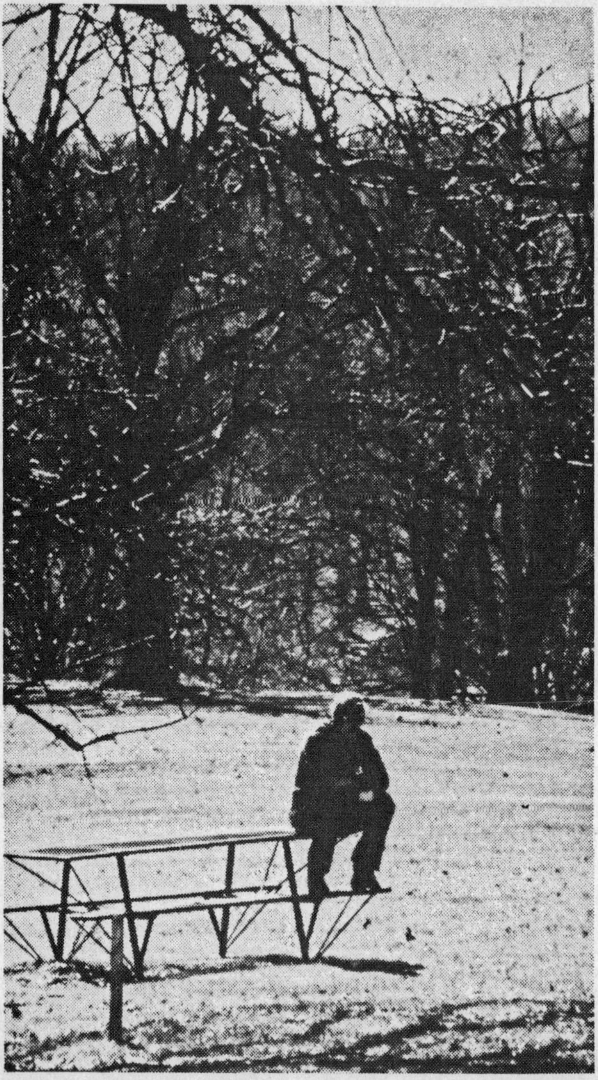

3
Stuck between the Good Times

Loneliness.

Every once in a while you remember what it feels like. Or maybe you feel it all the time; it sits there beside your other old friend called depression. It's a feeling of loss, like you've lost or are going to miss out on some valuable relationships. It's a feeling of not belonging, of no one understanding or caring. It's not being attached to anyone, not being accepted, feeling as if you've got nothing to offer, even when you are accepted.

Sometimes you'll hear people say that it's good to feel lonely. That it develops character, makes you self-sufficient and liberated. After all, the personal code of western civilization is to be independent and competitive, to cultivate individualism and personal freedom, right? The macho hero of the spy novel is a tough banana—he's never married, he's independent, he never commits himself to a relationship with anyone, and he relates to others only by choice and not because he needs to. He's a loner, and he's tough.

Loneliness stinks. Suzanne Gordon, author of *Lonely in America,* said, "To be alone is to be different, to be different is to be alone, and to be in the interior of this fatal circle is to be lonely."

What Is It?

Loneliness isn't just being alone. I remember times in school when I was glad to be sitting by myself near the end of the bus route so I could do some thinking or studying. Then there were other times when I would sit alone and *wish* somebody would sit with me. That was different.

Sometimes it's good to be alone. Sometimes the chance to hide away in your own room or hike over a hill by yourself is exactly what you need. Even Jesus Christ, the Man who lived a perfect life, was often found alone (Matthew 14:23; Luke 9:18, 36; John 6:15). Don't be concerned if you feel like getting away from the hassle of your 23 brothers and sisters! To want to be alone is fine, sometimes.

But when you're alone and feel *anxious* about being alone, then you're lonely. When you sit alone watching TV for five hours straight on Saturday night and you're upset about not having anyone to do anything with, you're lonely. When your folks get divorced and you lose your daily relationship with your dad, and you're isolated from him and feel sad/mad about it; you feel lonely. When you sit by yourself at lunchtime every day, and feel dumb about it—you're lonely.

So loneliness is being alone when you don't want to be. It comes in two nasty forms: social isolation and emotional isolation.

Social isolation produces a type of loneliness that's usually temporary. It's when you feel that you need a group of supporting friends, when you feel out on the fringe, floating aimlessly. Know the feeling? Social loneliness is often caused by circumstances.

Emotional isolation is more a result of emotional conflict. This kind of loneliness sinks into you even when all the circumstances in your life seem right. You're lonely because of what's going on inside your head. Familiar with this type of loneliness?

Let's look at the possible causes of loneliness in each of its forms. Then we'll see what can be done about the problem.

Three Stages

You go through three stages of development when you're most open to being attacked by loneliness. The first stage is as a youngster when you need the care and interaction of adults. A toddler needs authority figures who are interested in him, who care for him, who discipline him in love.

Loneliness can pop up even at this early stage if these basic needs aren't met. And in our present

54 / From Rock Bottom to Mountaintop

society, the odds are getting bigger that these early needs won't be met. In the United States, there'll be over a million divorces again this year. There are currently over 5 million families where a single parent is trying to meet the children's physical and emotional needs. There are over 7.5 million kids under the age of 18 who live in homes where divorce or separation have split up the parents. Thousands of illegitimate children were born last year, most to grow up with no father figure. And often, the youngsters who don't get stuck in *those* statistics are virtually left alone as Ma's and Pa's work schedules keep them away from home. A kid whose childhood needs for parental love aren't met is wide open to loneliness.

A second stage of development comes in early adolescence when a kid experiences the need for acceptance among others of his age. You know the story. You want others to think you're important, that you have something going for you. So you get really careful about which clothes you wear, how you do your hair, what kind of activities you get into. You've got a natural need for people to tell you that you're OK.

Loneliness haunts teenagers if this need for peer acceptance isn't met. It's a tough need to meet. When you're in high school and your family moves to a new town or you get into a new school, it's hard to be immediately accepted by all these new people who don't know you. Over 40 million American families move each year, so it's a good possibility that you have been or will be one of those

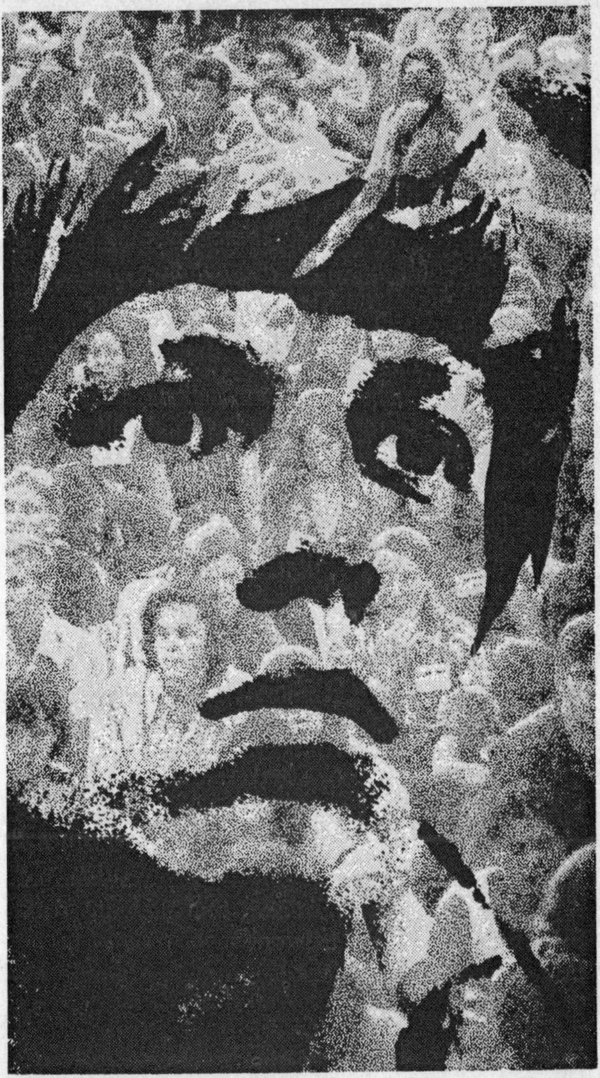

persons who goes through the misery of being the new kid in town.

The need to be accepted by peers is a tough bill to fill also because of our youth-oriented society's emphasis on the wrong value system. By that I mean most teenagers will easily accept another only if he's good looking or smart or athletically coordinated or talented. You could be a fantastic person, but if you're not good-looking, slow at algebra, a klutz at sports, and don't play lead guitar—people will be slow to accept you. And that's dumb. And that's why it's easy to feel lonely as a teenager— it's hard to feel accepted.

A third level of development opens another door for loneliness to get you by the throat. The stage of older adolescence—maybe college-age—is when the need for an intimate relationship with a person of the opposite sex often gets pretty strong. If the need isn't met, loneliness can step in with gusto.

We live in a society where low-budget ideas of love almost *destine* a person to loneliness. Our culture says that you're supposed to meet the "right one" about this time in your life. You're supposed to be attractive and lovable. You're supposed to be knowledgeable and experienced in sex relations. If you're still living by yourself with no one even on the horizon, there must be something wrong with you. You feel as if you're really missing out, as if nobody will ever want you. So if all these stupid myths are humiliating you, you're tempted to start focusing your interests on things rather than people. On careers and money and accomplishments to the exclusion of relationships. Because you get lonely.

Practical Reasons for Loneliness

Against that backdrop of the basic causes of loneliness in kids, here are a few practical reasons people your age get bloated with loneliness.

Jana's dad got a new job, and she and her family moved from Connecticut to Louisiana. The first day she attended her new school, not a single kid talked to her. The second day nobody said anything to her again except for the clod who said, "Hey, you-all talk funny."

Rob just broke up last week with Bea. And since he left his buddies when he started going with Bea, he hardly knows what to do with himself on Friday night.

This week everybody Beth knows took off to a camp up in the Sierras, and here she is stuck home baby-sitting her brother and sisters all week while her folks are out of town.

And you can think of more situations where the circumstances make you feel lonely. Factors that are usually beyond your control can make you feel like the loneliest person on earth.

But there are also practical reasons for loneliness that don't come from your circumstances. They come from you.

Curt walked up to the circle of guys around the pinball machine. He didn't know any of them. "Guess what two words have the most letters," he blurted. Nobody said anything. "The words are *post office!*" None of the guys smiled.

Jodie never seemed to be able to hang onto any friends. They always dropped her after a couple weeks. "I don't know what Lila has against me," she announced just before typing class. "All I did was give her a few ideas on how she could dress nicer. And that her hair looked bad the way it is. Big deal."

Gart Kulag apparently thought no one but Gart Kulag existed. He enjoyed himself most when he was with someone else who would let him talk about his stereo system and his Mustang and his dream of being a millionaire and his love of lasagna and his sore wrist. . . .

Sunny never felt as if she fit. She thought her name was dumb: Sunshine. And she didn't even have blonde hair. She was overweight, short, and had been in the slowest reading group in the fourth grade. Now a high school graduate, she had never been on a date, had never really *done* anything, and had no friends.

John was a senior in college. He started feeling desperate about not having a girlfriend. Everybody always said he was sharp—almost handsome, athletic, and fairly intelligent. But every time he'd get into a more-than-casual relationship with a girl, he'd get scared that she'd find out what he was *really* like. Then she'd probably drop him like a rotten watermelon. So he would drop her first. Time after time.

All these people are opening themselves up to

some pretty heavy loneliness. If they keep up their act, they'll be alone and won't like it because of things within themselves. They have areas they need to develop in their personalities or emotional conflicts.

But you don't *have* to be lonely on a permanent basis. Really. How do you kick the loneliness habit? Let's look first at what *not* to do when you're lonely.

The Don'ts of Loneliness

Don't sing, "Poor, poor pitiful me." If you start nursing your pain along, wallowing in it, it'll get worse.

Don't decide that you don't need anybody. God designed people to relate to others—"It is not good for the man to be alone" (Genesis 2:18). So don't give up on relationships, don't quit caring about people. Don't start living for things. Don't retreat from everybody—as if to punish them for not caring about you. ("They'll be sorry when I'm not around anymore!")

Don't generalize: "There's *nothing* I can do. It'll be this way the *rest of my life*. They're *all* creeps, anyway. *Nobody* cares about me. *Nobody* understands." You may feel that way, but none of these generalizations is true, regardless of who you are.

Don't start demanding attention. Don't read your assertiveness-training booklet and then try to force people to feel sorry for you because you're lonely. Don't manipulate other people to include you—you don't have a right to their time and friendship. Don't play sick just to get attention.

Don't pull the Great Escape. Some people do this by joining some weird cult or organization where they lose their identities. Some people try to escape loneliness by jumping into wrong relationships, such as a recent divorcee marrying the first guy she sees, such as a guy joining a street gang because there's nobody else to do anything with, such as a girl eloping with somebody she doesn't love just to escape a lonely home life. Some try to escape loneliness in booze or dope. And of course the biggest escape of all is suicide. But don't give up. There's hope.

What to Do about Loneliness

How do you step out of the feeling that you've either lost or won't ever have a rich relationship? You should cultivate rich relationships with others. Now, obviously that's the simple answer—we'll get to the complex answers in a minute. But write it down somewhere: Loneliness can't survive for long in a life filled with relationships.

Well, you say, that's the whole problem—no relationships! Right. So we're going to change that. Here's how anyone can cultivate relationships:

Value other people. The Bible puts it this way: "Do nothing from selfishness or empty conceit, but with humility of mind let each of you regard one another as more important than himself; do not merely look out for your own personal interests,

Stuck between the Good Times / 61

but also for the interests of others" (Philippians 2:3-4). The idea is to focus on others. There *are* people out there with whom you can strike up a relationship. Yeah, you say, but there's nobody who has my style or who is my age or who is friendly or who could be The Romance of My Life. Maybe. So drop your expectations. Even if the kid next door isn't as "sharp" as you are (in whose eyes?), he could end up being a deep friend. Maybe an elderly man or lady could fill a surprising cavity of need for fellowship in you. Who says you can't reach out to a person of the opposite sex unless he or she is a prime target for matrimony? Whoever the people around you are, they're valuable. God designed them as unique individuals, and they've got something to offer you! They're important, their needs are important, and you could be important to them.

Risk. Now, having that kind of biblical attitude is going to leave you in a risky position. If you befriend some homely kid who is lonelier than you are, other kids might start associating the two of you. They might ask, "Hey, what're you doing hanging around with that loser?" So you need to be brave. Of course, if you chicken out and drop the idea of ever relating to losers, you can always go back to loneliness. Deciding that you'll develop relationships with other people is also risky because you may get hurt. When you open yourself up to someone, there's always the possibility somewhere along the line that he'll reject you. So there are risks in developing relationships. But believe me, the risks are worth it.

62 / From Rock Bottom to Mountaintop

Effort. Thinking of others as more important than you are carries another price tag. It's not only risky; it takes effort. Let's say you feel lonely. So you purposely strike up a conversation with a kid in school or at work who you know doesn't have any friends. That night you're engrossed in a fantastic rerun of *Mork and Mindy* when the phone rings. It's your new friend who needs to talk out a problem with you. Now, if you want to beat this loneliness thing, if you want to develop relationships by thinking of the value of others, what will you have to do? You'll have to stay on the phone, listening intently and sharing with your new acquaintance—rather than hanging up as quickly as you can and returning to the TV. It takes effort to build relationships. It takes a constant refusal to give in to selfishness, to live as if you're the only important person alive.

Ideas. Now for some dumb, practical ideas. How do you start reaching out? When you realize that people don't have to be rated "choice," that they're *all* valuable, what do you do? You start a letter-writing schedule with people you used to know—maybe even the ones you used to think weren't important. You visit every elderly person around to see if he needs any help in the yard or house, and you talk and listen to him. You gather your courage and sit next to somebody who sits by him/herself during your lunchtime and start with a line such as, "Hi I don't think I've met you before my name's Ichabod Housermountain. Most people call me Icky for short." You write a letter to your dad because you never see him much, asking him what it was

Stuck between the Good Times / 63

like when he was your age—back when everyone still spoke Latin and dressed in togas. You take your youth group absentee list and call somebody to see if you can give him a ride to church. You send a note to somebody who's going through a rough time. You offer to help with a kids' club. You visit people at a rest home. Etc.

You see, the people you develop relationships with may not all be "ideal" people. But you as a human being are pocked with lots of blank spaces called needs. And you never know who is going to fill one of those blank spaces. A friendship with an old, old man or a little snot-nosed kid can fill up one of those spaces that used to be full of loneliness.

That's it. Quit focusing on yourself. Go ahead and think about other people. In all the risk and all the effort, reach out to cultivate relationships with anyone you can get hold of.

If this sounds too simplistic, good. It was supposed to be simple. Now for some complexities. Sometimes you feel so overwhelmed by loneliness you just can't muster the initiative to reach out. It's just not in you. What then?

The Complexities

When feelings of loneliness seem to knock you flat and you just *can't* jump out and start developing new relationships, you've got to put on your thinking cap. "Teach me good discernment and knowledge" (Psalm 119:66) should be your prayer. Your task is to figure out the cause of your loneliness. Your discernment will pinpoint one of two types of causes: circumstantial or personal.

Circumstantial. Remember when we talked about loneliness sprouting up in you when you've just moved, when you've gone through the loss of a close relationship through death or breakup, when you're forced to miss out on a special occasion? That's often a time when feelings of loneliness squash you so badly that you have to look up to ground level. Here's a "to-do" list for those times:

• Accept the fact that you're lonely. It's not weak or effeminate to admit that you're homesick or that you feel lost. Loneliness is a usual response to many circumstances. Accept it as a natural, temporary reaction to your loss. Don't panic. It won't last.

• Relish your relationship with the Lord. These times might be just what you need to drive you toward a fresh fellowship with God. Even in your temporary loneliness, He's with you: "The Lord your God is with you wherever you go" (Joshua 1:9); "When you pass through the waters, I will be with you" (Isaiah 43:2); "I will never desert you, nor will I ever forsake you" (Hebrews 13:5); also see Psalm 23:4; John 8:16; 16:32.

• Remember that other Christians care too. "If we walk in the light as He Himself is in the light, we have fellowship with one another" (1 John 1:7). Regardless of circumstances, regardless of feelings, fellow believers who are walking in the light—walking in the Spirit—care. They may not be able to *do* anything, but they care.

- Then, as soon as you can get your Spirit-controlled act together, start on the key to erasing loneliness. Develop new relationships.

Personal. Maybe you feel you just can't cultivate new relationships, but your God-given discernment reveals that the reasons are not circumstantial. There are no external causes that keep you feeling lonely. Then, probably, you've got some personal projects to work on. Remember the guy with the dumb post office joke? The critical girl? Gart Kulag who couldn't talk about anything but himself? The girl whose name was Sunny, only she never felt like it? And the guy who wouldn't get close in a relationship? Well, as you noticed, that mob has some problems to work out before they'll enjoy relationships that'll dispel their loneliness. Let's see what a person can do in this brand of loneliness:

- Realize that your feelings of loneliness point out a problem area. Something in you needs development. Loneliness can be a useful signal to warn of problems, since it gets our attention so completely—it hurts. So when it hurts, it's telling you something. It's helping you focus on a problem to work through. Do some self-examination, ask your pastor, ask the Lord to help you determine what the problem is. Write it down so this problem that's promoting your loneliness is clear to you.

- Change what you can change. Lose weight if you can. Fix your hair a new way. And don't overlook the obvious. One of the nicest guys I've ever known had no close friends. I wasn't a close friend probably for the same reason all his other acquaint-

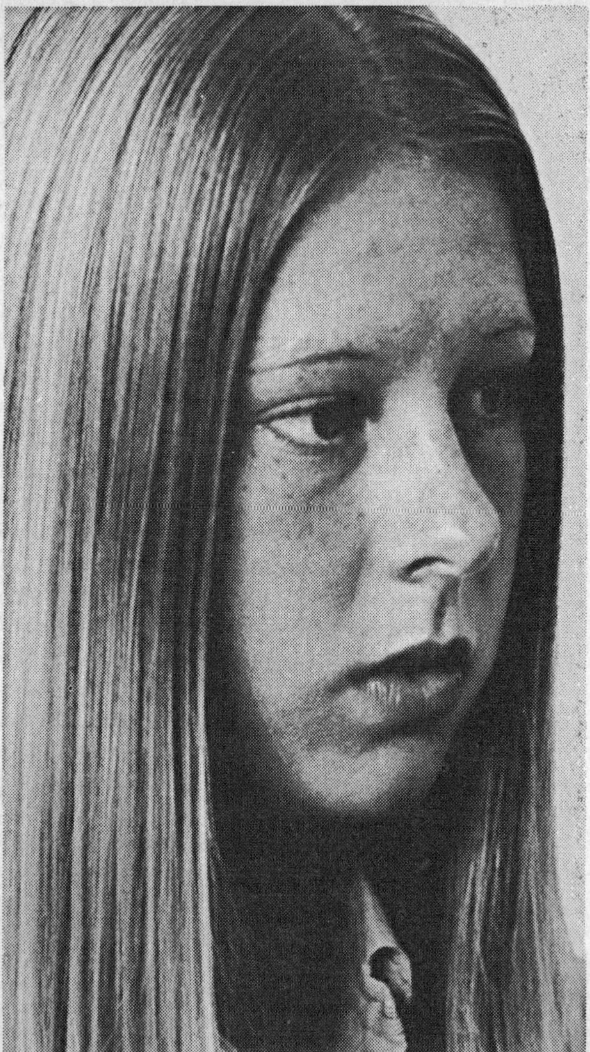

ances weren't—the guy reeked. His dorm room at college was pig city. If I'd had more maturity then, I would have explained to him that he'd probably never have a lonely day in his life if he'd learn to shower and use that newfangled thing called a deodorant. So go ahead. Spruce up your old body. Get crazy, buy yourself a toothbrush. You don't have to be stinky or messy.

Other things that may promote your lonely outlook can be changed. The example of the guy with the post office joke should tell you that there are ways that work and ways that don't work as you relate to people. Work on your social skills. Read some books; get some advice. You can actually learn to correct poor social habits.

Personal qualities can be changed if they're holding you back from enjoying real relationships. Are you sarcastic, critical, cynical, destructive in what you say? Are you a snob, conceited, selfish, holier-than-thou, or rude? Do you hog conversations, bore people to death, talk all the time? People don't like to be around people like that. But you, with God's help, don't have to *be* like that. You *can* develop qualities of love, joy, peace, patience, kindness, goodness, faithfulness, gentleness, and self-control (Galatians 5:22-23). Nobody runs from a person like that!

- Accept what you can't change. Face it, maybe you can't do anything about a personal trait that contributes to a lonely outlook. Maybe you feel your appearance or lack of abilities is forcing you to be lonely. Maybe you were born with what others call

68 / From Rock Bottom to Mountaintop

a "deformity." Maybe you don't like the shape of your face. Maybe you have a speech impediment that can't be corrected. Maybe you're permanently stuck in a wheelchair. Now, none of these things *keeps* you from being able to enjoy relationships, but maybe they make you *feel* that you just can't reach out.

When you feel bad about yourself, you're usually oversensitive to other people's reactions. A girl who feels unattractive might constantly think, *What are they thinking about me?* while meeting someone. Instead she could be thinking about the *other* person. Clarence, who feels he's not worth much because he can't get high grades, works at cutting down everybody else in order to make himself look better. So he has no friends.

What do you do when you feel bad about something you can't change? Work through the following exercises, and we'll figure it out:

Where do you feel you don't rate? Jot down how you feel about:
   your intelligence
   your talents
   your appearance
   your body
   your sexuality
   your skills
   your spiritual life
   your ability to be sociable

Now why do you feel that way? Let's say Jake feels bad about his appearance; his parents are from

Stuck between the Good Times / 69

different races. He thinks that the standard attitude is that it's not good to look like a racially mixed person. So he decides that he's not all right. As a result he keeps to himself—withdrawing from relationships.

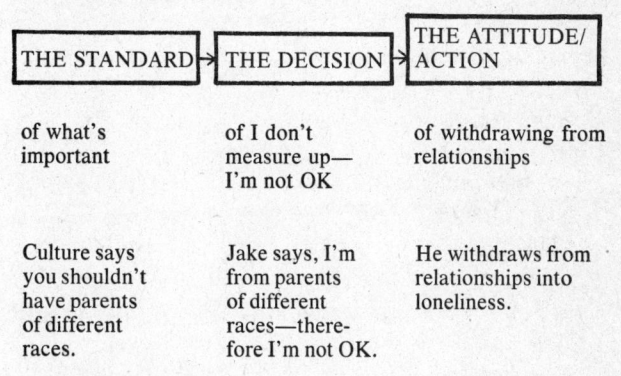

THE STANDARD →	THE DECISION →	THE ATTITUDE/ ACTION
of what's important	of I don't measure up— I'm not OK	of withdrawing from relationships
Culture says you shouldn't have parents of different races.	Jake says, I'm from parents of different races—therefore I'm not OK.	He withdraws from relationships into loneliness.

There are *standards* that give you messages about what's important in a person, and you *decide* if you're OK or not by whether you measure up to these standards. Then your *attitudes and actions* of reaching out to others result from your OK or not-OK decision.

What are some of the *standards* pushed by the media (TV, movies, magazines, etc.) in our culture?

What should the ideal teenage girl look like?
What should the ideal teenage guy look like?
What should girls be good at?
What should guys be good at?
Describe the girl who attracts guys.
Describe the guy who attracts girls.
You see, our cultural system says it's extremely

70 / From Rock Bottom to Mountaintop

important to be the right size, shape, and color. You're supposed to have clear skin, fine facial features, talent, coordination (especially for guys). You should often date, always be involved in rowdy, exciting, expensive activities. In fact, the standard is so set in our culture that jokes are especially funny when they're about ugliness or an imperfect body shape or a lack of intelligence.

Miss America is supposed to be the perfect example of the female American, right? And Mr. America the male. What are the standards by which each is chosen?

These standards have barraged us all as children through the media. When echoed by an authority figure in our life, the standards *really* affect us. Any of these childhood messages sound familiar?

You're plain; you sure won't be attractive.

You can't do *anything* right, can you?

You're so dumb.

We never really wanted you anyway. We wanted a baby of the opposite sex.

You're so uncoordinated it's unbelievable.

Think carefully through:

When you were little, what was the worst thing ever said or done to you?

Be aware of the pain or anger you felt then.

How and when do you experience that feeling now?

What were typical things said about you?

What were you told you'd end up as?

How do these childhood messages affect the way you feel about yourself now?

Stuck between the Good Times / 71

By the time a child is eight years old, most of the messages of his childhood have taken root. A child may be told that he doesn't measure up to the cultural standard of smartness, that he's dumb. All these messages, based on all these standards (good looks, intelligence, coordination, etc.), add up to one big message: You're supposed to be like everyone else. You're supposed to conform to the cultural standard.

God's standards are different from most of our cultural standards. So His messages, given in the Bible, are mostly different from the ones we've been hearing all our lives. God says it's not really important what a person looks like on the outside (1 Samuel 16:7). God designed your body as a unique, special creation. Nobody's the same. All are unique, from fingerprints to facial features (Psalm 139:14-16; Isaiah 45:9; Romans 9:20). God says an attractive person is one who has developed qualities such as love and joy and patience. (Compare the qualities mentioned in Galatians 5:22-23 with the attractive men and women of the Bible.) God says inner qualities are far more important than what's on the outside (1 Peter 3:3-4).

Now the real question comes up: Which set of standards are you going to believe when you decide what's important in a person? Will you believe the world's standards? Is it possible that they and your childhood messages about them are false? Does every movie star who is fantastically good-looking and rich and intelligent and athletic *really* have rich relationships? Does every Beautiful Person always

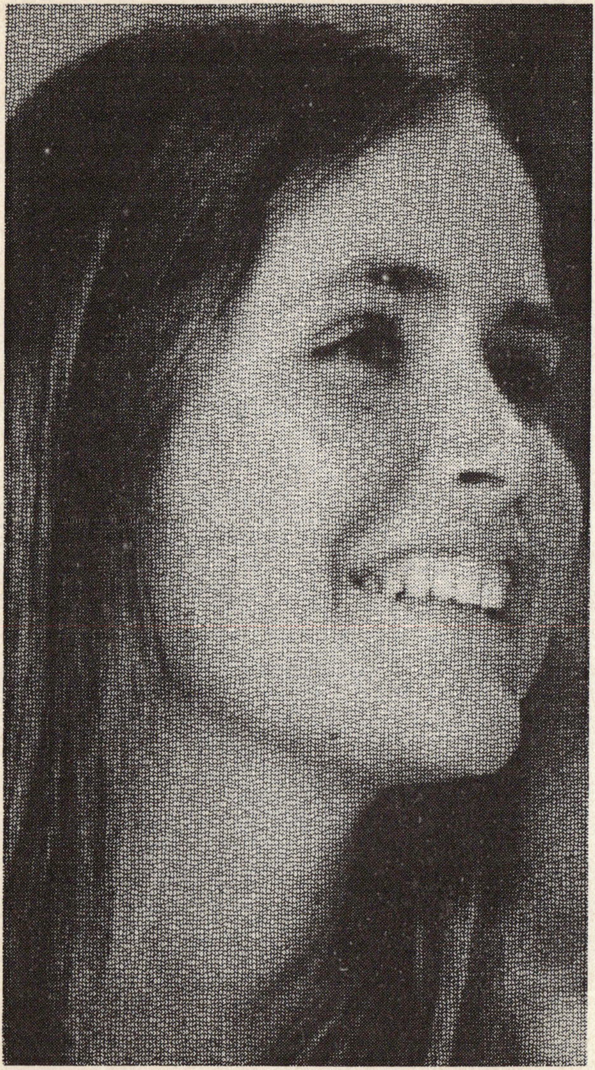

Stuck between the Good Times / 73

enjoy beautiful relationships? Or are those standards false?

You can choose to believe what God, the Designer of life, says. You can trust that His standards, His messages are true!

Decisions are based on your standards. You use a standard to decide if you're OK or not. Maybe some of the decisions you've made about yourself include:

I'll never amount to anything.

I'm stupid.

I can't do anything right.

I'm not important.

I don't deserve to live.

I should have been the opposite sex.

I'm ugly.

My body is disgusting.

All of these decisions add up to one big *I'm not OK.* They're *all* based on cultural standards. And they all contribute directly to the conclusion: *Since I'm not OK, I don't want anybody getting close enough to find out. So I won't develop any relationships. I'll be lonely.*

If, on the other hand, you can decide that you're *OK* by using the *true* standards of life—God's standards—then you've got something to offer. You can think: *It's OK for people to get close. It's all right for me to reveal who I am!*

Your attitudes and actions are determined by your decisions about yourself, right? Think through how the different sets of standards eventually affect your relationships:

74 / From Rock Bottom to Mountaintop

THE STANDARD →	THE DECISION →	THE ATTITUDE/ ACTION
You're supposed get A's.	I get D's, so I'm not OK.	I'm ashamed when people find out I'm dumb, so I withdraw.
OR		
You're God-designed to use God's wisdom; your IQ doesn't matter (1 Corinthians 1:26-31).	My intelligence level is OK.	I'm intelligent enough for who I am; I'm free to let people get to know me!
You're supposed to be good-looking like the models and stars.	I'm really plain —I'm not OK.	People only want sharp looking friends. I quit on relationships.
OR		
God planned your body's features (Psalm 139:13-15).	I must look OK— who am I to knock the Master of the Universe! I look fine to Him!	I can forget about looks and concentrate on how to be loving, not just lovable.
You're supposed to have a clear complexion.	My acne problem isn't acceptable —I'm not OK.	I'm going to stay out of sight till I'm 30!
OR		
Outside blemishes are bothersome but aren't important to relationships.	My acne problem is no fun, but that's all right —I'm OK.	I'll concentrate that much more on *others*.

Stuck between the Good Times / 75

So! Let's sum up where we are. Loneliness will be prolonged if you feel you can't develop relationships. You may feel that way because you've decided you're not OK—there's something wrong that you can't change. You've decided you're not OK because you don't match up to the cultural standard. But the cultural standard, you've just realized, can be totally false!

Now. How do you accept what you can't change?

Rediscover the true standards of what's important in a person. Submerge yourself in God's way of thinking in the Bible. Don't allow your thinking to be conformed to the world's standards, but let God *renew* your mind! (Romans 12:2)

Work on a single area at a time, starting with the most painful. For instance, if the reason you don't reach out in relationships is because of your height, examine results of the standards in chart form:

THE STANDARD	THE DECISION	THE ATTITUDE/ ACTION
Girls should be shorter; guys should be taller.	I'm not the right height—I'm not O.K.	I might as well give up on relationships—nobody'll want me.

OR

God doesn't put any importance whatsoever on height.	Whatever height God gives me is OK!	I can quit being concerned about my height and start enjoying relationships with others, regardless of *their* height.

76 / From Rock Bottom to Mountaintop

• *Rewrite the "message" you listen to.* Actually write on 3" x 5" cards what God's true standards tell you. For instance: "My height is no accident (Psalm 139:15)." Stick the cards in your textbooks, on your mirrors. Reprogram your thinking according to God's standards.

- *Redecide your evaluation of yourself.* As you constantly remind yourself of the message of God's standards, you'll be able to actually decide: "With God as my Designer, I'm OK!"
- *Finally, recommit yourself to developing new relationships.* Directed by God's Holy Spirit, get back to this key in erasing loneliness. Develop those relationships!

And in Summary

Whew! We've come a long way in this chapter. Let's look at what we've covered:

- Loneliness is being alone and feeling upset about it.
- Loneliness creeps in most easily when childhood needs for parenting, adolescent needs of peer acceptance, and young adult needs of intimacy aren't met.
- Loneliness can be caused temporarily by circumstances or more permanently by personal conflicts.
- Loneliness can't survive where relationships are being built.

And finally, if you feel overwhelmed by loneliness and can't even *begin* to sort out the causes, maybe a professional counselor or your pastor can help. Don't be lonely.

Guilt

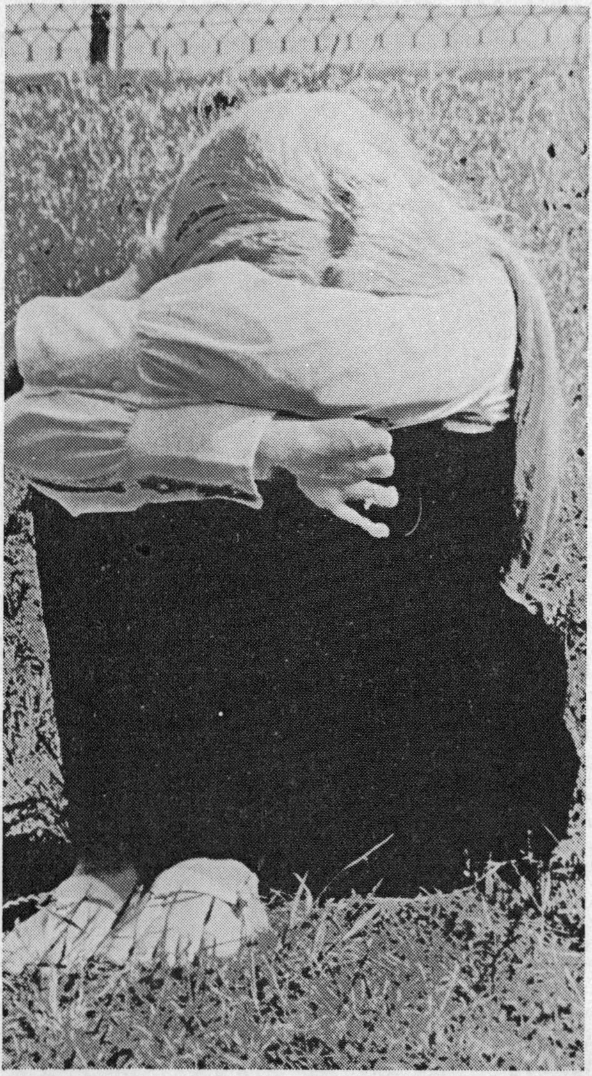

4
The Squeeze You Can't Avoid

Jennifer first felt the guilt in her throat. Like Pepto-Bismol it coated her inside from her neck to her stomach. And by the time her parents got home she felt sure it was visibly oozing out from every pore of her body.

"Jennifer?" He'd called just after her folks had left.

"Yeah, John."

"I'm coming over."

"Can't. My folks are gone, so you're not supposed to."

"Who'll ever know? Be there in five minutes."

John arrived, and they watched an old rerun of "Gunsmoke" as he massaged her back and tickled her earlobes. The thick excitement that ensued was not due to the exploits of Matt Dillon and Miss Kitty on TV. And now Jennifer had to deceive her parents

82 / From Rock Bottom to Mountaintop

as to what she'd been doing all evening: being way too free with her body.

Jennifer felt sick. Grimy. Guilty.

Clancey knew all the tricks. He'd been developing the art since third grade. He'd tried stashing a page of notes behind the towel dispenser in the little boys' room, then asking halfway through the test if he could go to the rest room. He'd outfitted an old watch with a disc of tiny notes, so when he turned the little knob the answers would show in the day and date openings. He'd written theorems and hypotheses on the edges and soles of his tennis shoes, inscribed important history dates on his pencil, and wrote French vocabulary words on his fingernails. Occasionally he resorted to the more mundane practices of slipping a page of notes from his pocket, writing answers on the chalkboard before a test session in hopes the teacher wouldn't notice, and even looking at another kid's paper. Clancey's next project was a system for the biology test. It was taking him hours of concentrated research to decide whether to plant a miniature answer sheet under the dissected frog's liver or to record the answers and then during the test play them back through an earplug on his pocket cassette recorder.

It was fun to Clancey. Wrong? Sure, but everybody was doing it. And it couldn't have been too bad; he never felt guilty. Never.

Stan was a two-year-old Christian when his parents sat him down and mumbled, "We're filing for

The Squeeze You Can't Avoid / 83

divorce, Stan." It was just that simple and that much of a surprise. It felt like like the bottom of his stomach caved in.

That night he had to talk with somebody, and Arnie was the only Christian guy around. "It's probably my fault," Stan started out.

"What is?" Arnie was working on his VW dune buggy.

"The whole thing."

"Well, whatever it is, you're not supposed to be so down-in-the-mouth, Stan. You're supposed to 'count it all joy,' remember?"

Stan didn't answer.

"Yeah, you seem really glum lately. Don't you know it's a sin for a Christian to worry? You're supposed to be happy all the time, Stan."

"OK, OK. So I'm a Christian, but I still feel lousy. Don't *you* ever worry or feel guilty?" Stan said, staring directly at Arnie, a defiant look in his eyes.

"Yeah, I feel guilty all right." I don't know what about, but I feel guilty sometimes. Make you happy?" Arnie almost yelled the words as Stan walked away.

Guilt is a universal feeling. Everybody senses it, and everybody seeks some method to get rid of it—because it's painful. Why does the Nicaraguan girl crawl on her bare knees up the raspy stone steps of the local cathedral? What keeps millions of people on the appointment rosters of psychiatrists, psychologists, and counselors? What makes you feel ugly after you take part in something you feel is really wrong? Why did Jesus Christ get nailed on a cross? Guilt.

Guilt is one of the heaviest factors in the scale of human emotions. So there's a lot to be thought through about it—such as, why is there guilt? How do you distinguish between real guilt and false guilt? Is guilt a good thing? How do you handle guilt?

You don't have to be a throat-slicing, old-lady-kicking, criminal-type to know about guilt. A lot of people think guilt comes only as a result of the wrong things you *do*. But what you *do* is a result of what you *are*. Let's look first at guilt as a result of who you are: a being with an imperfect human nature.

Human Nature and Guilt

About 3:00 A.M. I jerked awake to realize I had strayed over the centerline. I swung the truck back into my lane just in time to see a hitch-hiker huddled alonside the road. *Maybe I'll get him talking to keep me awake,* I thought. So I pulled over and opened the door as he came stumbling up. And he kept me awake.

"I'm coming back from L. A.," he said, starting his monologue. "I been out there for three weeks just trying to get into things, you know. The groups, the people into God. But they didn't have it, so I'm going back home. I've got it all anyway. Oh, excuse me for not introducing myself. My name is Jesus Christ." He didn't smile as he offered a handshake.

"I'm perfect, you see. So I don't need any of that."

We sat in silence while I tried to figure out what to say next.

He turned, "Don't have any cigarettes on you, do you?"

"Don't smoke," I said. "You mean you smoke?"

"Yeah. Gotta have one pretty soon. I'm getting jittery. Haven't had a smoke in two days." He rubbed his hands nervously.

"I thought you were perfect."

"Oh, I am."

"But that would mean you'd be perfectly complete. You wouldn't need anything. Like cigarettes."

"Don't confuse me, man," he snarled. "Just don't confuse me."

It's true, friends and neighbors. Man is not perfect. He isn't complete in himself. He has needs. He gets confused. He has imperfections. He *is* imperfect. Anyone disagreeing with that has either a regular breakfast of angel dust or an IQ of -15. The Bible says, "There is none righteous, not even one. . . . There is none who does good; there is not even one" (Romans 3:10, 12).

Every human is born with an imperfect nature—he inherits it from his imperfect parents who inherited their imperfect natures from their imperfect parents and so on back to old Adam and Eve. The Bible points out that Adam was the first human to sing, "I was sinking deep in sin—whoopee!" And since every human is genetically descended from Adam, his sin nature was passed out to everybody: "The result of one trespass was condemnation for all men . . . through the disobedience of the one man the many were made sinners" (Romans 5:18-19, NIV). Again, the Bible states that "all have sinned and fall short of the glory of God" (Romans 3:23). Face it, we're all in this imperfection thing together. We're all sinners.

The problem. God is perfect. Man isn't perfect. He's born in sin (Psalm 51:5). God and man aren't together, since perfection doesn't include imperfection. There's something wrong in the relationship between man and the God who made him. And when there's something wrong, there is guilt. When there's guilt, there is a consequence: "For the wages of sin is death" (Romans 6:23). This death, spiritual death, means to be separated forever from the life of God.

When you look at the whole "problem of the human condition" in this way, doesn't it make you want to say, "But it's not fair! So Adam liked fruit salads; why blame me? I don't want to be guilty"? Modern philosophers call this problem *existential guilt*—a vague sense of guilt that comes from simply *being*.

The gap between man and God produces guilt. Not that every human *feels* guilty. He *is* guilty. Just as a speeder is guilty whether or not he feels guilty doing 50 MPH in a 20 MPH hospital zone. And guilt demands consequences. The guilty speeder has to pay a fine or spend a few days vacationing in the county jail. The embezzler who is found guilty must pay the consequences: 10 years in the state pen. Guilt demands payment. So the consequence of

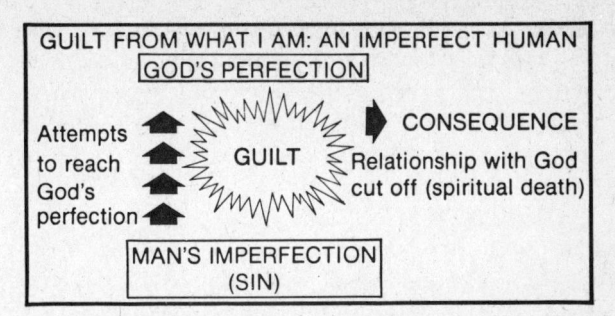

> GUILT FROM WHAT I AM: AN IMPERFECT HUMAN
> GOD'S PERFECTION
> Attempts to reach God's perfection → GUILT ← Relationship with God cut off (spiritual death) CONSEQUENCE
> MAN'S IMPERFECTION (SIN)

man's sinfulness is to exist in spiritual death, to be cut off from God forever.

The alternative. But once the payment is made, the offender is no longer guilty, right? After the speeder has lounged in jail for three days, the jailer opens the cell door and says, "You're free to go now. The sentence is fulfilled. Justice has been satisfied." That's if the speeder has an eloquent jailer. The idea is, once the penalty has been paid, the whole situation is put right. In fact, that's the meaning of the biblical term "justified"—"put right."

"The wages of sin is death, but the free gift of God is eternal life in Christ Jesus our Lord" (Romans 6:23). Jesus Christ offers man freedom from guilt because He paid the consequences that man deserves. He died. "God demonstrates His own love toward us, in that while we were yet sinners, Christ died for us" (Romans 5:8). The consequence of man's sin nature is eternal death. But Jesus' death paid the consequences for all mankind's guilt. When He cried, "My God, My God, why have You forsaken Me?" (Mark 15:34, NIV), Jesus was somehow separated from the other members of the Trinity. He experienced the spiritual death all mankind would have to go through. He paid the sentence, took care of the fine, made Himself an offering to take care of our guilt:

Surely our griefs He Himself bore,
And our sorrows He carried;
Yet we ourselves esteem Him stricken,
Smitten of God, and afflicted.
But He was pierced through for our
   transgressions,
He was crushed for our iniquities;
The chastening for our well-being fell on Him,
And by His scourging we are healed.
....

But the Lord was pleased
To crush Him, putting Him to grief;
If He would render Himself as a guilt offering,
. . . the Righteous One,
My Servant, will justify the many
As He will bear their iniquities (Isaiah 53:4-5, 10-11).

Adam gave us all a "gift"—a sinful human nature. Nice guy, huh? But Christ gave us all another gift: "And the gift is not like that which came through the one who sinned; for on the one hand the judgment arose from one transgression resulting in condemnation, but on the other hand the free gift arose from many transgressions resulting in justification" (Romans 5:16). Jesus paid it all. He made it right. He offers justification as a gift.

But like any gift, a person has to reach out and

receive it before it is his. It's as if you were busted for shoplifting a tuba and the judge, because of your guilt, sentenced you to 80 days in jail or payment of $43,819. The next day I come in to get you out—because I feel sorry for somebody so dumb as to try hiding a tuba under a coat—and pay the $43,819. The fine is paid, justice has been satisfied, you've been justified. But you're a little weird. You say, "Hey, nobody's going to make *me* a charity case. I refuse to accept that Stearns guy's payment. I'm going to pay it all myself!" So there you sit for another 79 days, paying off the consequences of your guilt when you could be free.

Now you're not really quite that dumb. But some people are when it comes to accepting Christ's payment of the consequence of their sin. They seem to say, "Well, that's nice that Jesus went to all that trouble for me, but I'd rather pay off this penalty of eternal spiritual death myself." So they go tripping off to an eternity without God because they refuse to receive Christ as the One who already paid their fine, who was the perfect Offering for their guilt!

If a person receives Christ as the One who died for him, God declares that person justified, "put right." God Himself steps into the person's life as Lord, and salvation (being saved from a godless eternity to life with Him) provides the alternative to guilt's consequence. The alternative is an incredible relationship with God.

The Bible says, "If you confess with your mouth Jesus as Lord, and believe in your heart that God raised Him from the dead, you shall be saved" (Romans 10:9). Have you made a decision to make Jesus your Lord, believing that He's alive after dying for your sin? Now is as good a time as any to make sure you've made the choice. It's the one big step you can take to solve your basic problem of guilt. You can have, through Christ, the foundation you need to handle the nitty-gritty guilt problems of everyday life—guilt that comes from what you *do*.

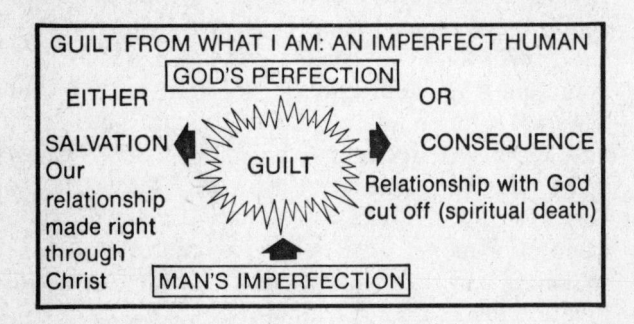

```
GUILT FROM WHAT I AM: AN IMPERFECT HUMAN
                 GOD'S PERFECTION
      EITHER                          OR
      SALVATION  ←    GUILT    →  CONSEQUENCE
      Our                             Relationship with God
      relationship                    cut off (spiritual death)
      made right
      through
      Christ     MAN'S IMPERFECTION
```

Guilt and Human Behavior

Now we're getting down to the practical problems of guilt. When you mess around too much in a physical relationship with somebody, you'll often feel the same guilt Jennifer did in the opening of this chapter. Or maybe you don't feel guilty even though you know you've done something wrong, as our man Clancey did. Or like Stan, maybe other people lay a false guilt on you—you feel bad but aren't sure why.

Let's think through typical ways people handle guilt. Then we'll see how a Christian, who has been given an official "right standing" with God, can handle the daily grind of the sin/guilt/sin/guilt cycle of normal human emotions.

Suicide. The no-nonsense approach to overwhelming guilt is to stretch out prone on a runway at O'Hare International Airport. Suicide is the second leading cause of death among young people. Some suicides arise from intense loneliness, some from simple despair, but many from guilt.

Don't think I'm just referring here to unchurched people. I'd guess that nearly every youth between 12 and 25 has thought about suicide, and probably one in five Christian kids has fantasized a plan of how to do it. When the problems get complicated and you feel sick and guilty, you're normal if you have the thought, "Oh, I wish I were dead." Maybe you feel that way right now. But escaping from life is definitely not the way to handle guilt.

Mind games. Some people are adept at figuring out new ways for handling guilt. One of the more popular methods is called "Lower the Standard." If the standard for human behavior is too high, just work it down a few notches.

Joe "New Morality" Smith likes premarital sex. It's fun. But it also makes him feel guilty after each episode. You see, Joe was taught that sexual relations outside marriage are wrong, that God's standard is: Enjoy sex only in marriage. Joe doesn't *want* to feel guilty. It's no fun. So he convinces himself that the standard should be adjusted a little

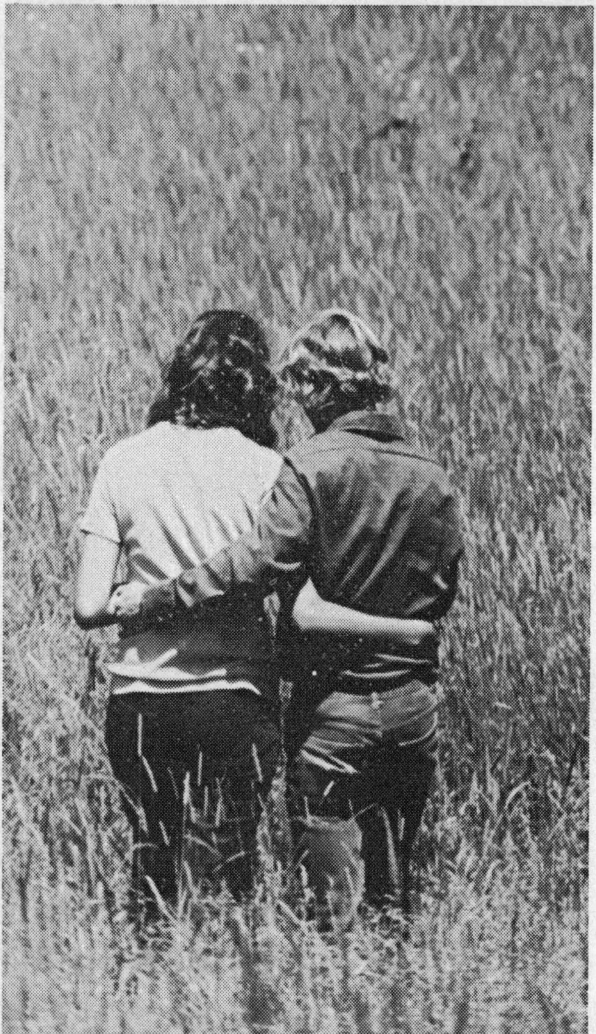

The Squeeze You Can't Avoid / 93

lower to: Enjoy sex as long as it doesn't hurt anybody. And what do you know? Under the new, lowered standard, Joe is doing what's right! He's enjoying sex but not hurting anybody! And, of course, when you're doing the *right* thing you shouldn't have to feel guilty.

The method works in all sorts of situations. When the sign says 55 MPH and I'm doing 75, I can tell myself: "Self, the law says to obey the speed limit, but they don't *really* expect you to go 55 on this freeway; it was designed for 80 MPH. And think about how everybody passed you when you were staying at 55—you looked dumb. The limit really *should* be 75, just the speed I'm traveling!" But when the red lights flash and the citation is signed, no amount of mind games will keep me from being guilty. Right?

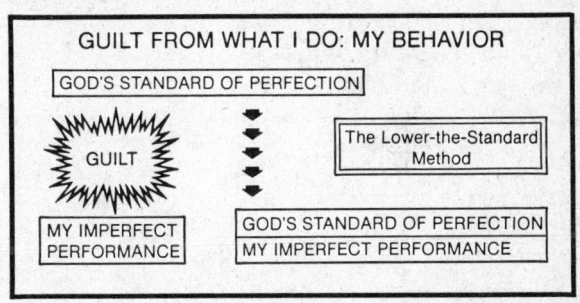

GUILT FROM WHAT I DO: MY BEHAVIOR

GOD'S STANDARD OF PERFECTION

GUILT ➤➤➤➤➤ The Lower-the-Standard Method

MY IMPERFECT PERFORMANCE | GOD'S STANDARD OF PERFECTION / MY IMPERFECT PERFORMANCE

See how the system works? There's no room left for guilt in between what I do and what I'm supposed to do! A variation of the theme is "Remove the Standard." In other words, just say that God and His standards don't exist, then *nothing* causes

94 / From Rock Bottom to Mountaintop

guilt! Everything's right and nothing's wrong!

The problem with the "Lower the Standard" and "Remove the Standard" methods of dealing with guilt is that they're just imaginary. They're mind games. In order to remove the guilt problem you *have* to pretend that God doesn't exist and you *have* to believe that rights or wrongs are just human creations.

But since the Bible says otherwise, a person could play all the mind games in his repertoire—maybe even numbing the *feeling* of guilt—and still *be* guilty in God's book.

Improved performance. This is a religious-sounding way to work at the guilt problem of doing the wrong things. The idea is simply to do a little better. Well, actually, to do a *lot* better. If lowering the standard didn't work, maybe raising the performance level will! If my imperfect performance level were nailed right up under God's standard of perfection, again there'd be no room for guilt!

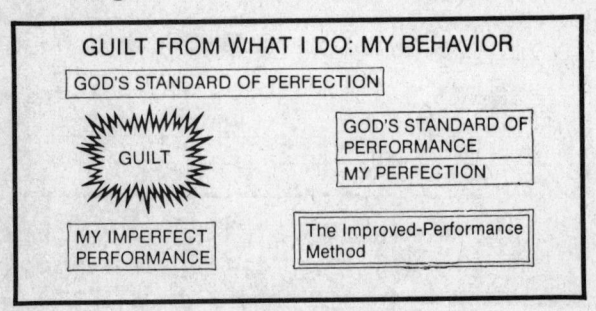

```
GUILT FROM WHAT I DO: MY BEHAVIOR
  GOD'S STANDARD OF PERFECTION

      GUILT                   GOD'S STANDARD OF
                              PERFECTION
                              MY PERFECTION

  MY IMPERFECT           The Improved-Performance
  PERFORMANCE            Method
```

Cults are big on this system of guilt removal. They claim you can actually become in this lifetime a perfected being, one with the Cosmic Force of the universe. And if it were possible, you would no longer have guilt problems!

Christians and pseudo-Christians like this method. In fact many religious leaders use guilt itself in forcing people to use this guilt-reducing plan! "Is God happy with the way you've been acting this week? Of course not! Some of you weren't at Sunday School this morning! Have you read your Bible every day? Do you have the testimony you should at your job or at school?"

The idea is to make the congregation feel guiltier than ever. Then, hopefully, they'll feel so badly that they'll shape up next week. Every guilty one of them will show up for Sunday School; they'll read three verses every day, like it or not; and they'll blurt out some noninspired-by-the-Spirit "testimony" to fellow workers or schoolmates.

Will they feel better? Probably. Will they *be* any less guilty? Probably not, since they're trying to improve their actions for the wrong reasons. Sunday School attendance may go up, but the level of Bible understanding will probably be as low as ever. Everyone will be able to say he read his Bible every day, but perhaps few will actually hear what God says to them. People will be out witnessing in the community, but it will be mostly human-powered rather than Spirit-powered. Improving performance is an empty way of dealing with guilt. Besides, it doesn't work.

Though a Spirit-controlled believer will find that his behavior improves as he matures spiritually, he'll never arrive at a perfection level till he steps into eternity. So, for sure, guilt-induced, human-controlled behavior will never even get close to perfection. Those claiming to have reached a level of perfection this side of eternity need to study passages such as 1 John 1:8, 10: "If we say that we have no sin, we are deceiving ourselves, and the truth is not in us. . . . If we say that we have not sinned, we make Him a liar, and His Word is not in us."

Trying to remove guilt by acting better doesn't work.

Self-punishment. Wrongdoing in thought, attitude, or action produces guilt. Guilt demands a consequence, a penalty. So sometimes people figure that the way to ease guilt's hold on their lives is to take over the job of providing the penalty. They punish themselves in order to remove the guilt caused by something they've done. They think a just punishment for fouling up their marriage relationship is to die the death of an alcoholic. They figure that since they played around with premarital sex, they should punish themselves by not allowing themselves to marry.

Penance, self-denial, and ridiculous self-sacrifice are often attempts to provide appropriate consequences for guilt.

Do you see the mistake of self-punishment as a guilt-removal method? Though the wrongdoer has taken on himself a self-inflicted consequence, guilt still remains! That's because regardless of how nasty a self-punishment the wrongdoer conjures up (maybe

I'll boil my big toe in oil and squash all the ants in my ant farm!), it's God who forgives wrong. When God's law is broken, He is the One to decide on how the resulting guilt is handled.

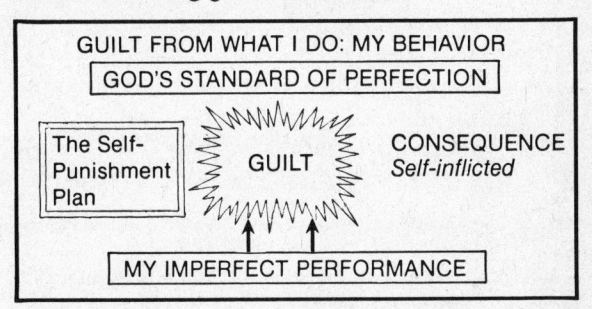

```
GUILT FROM WHAT I DO: MY BEHAVIOR
  GOD'S STANDARD OF PERFECTION

 The Self-                          CONSEQUENCE
 Punishment      GUILT              Self-inflicted
 Plan

  MY IMPERFECT PERFORMANCE
```

Playing God is tough. That's why none of these systems works. If God's standard of behavior has been broken, then *God* has a method to handle the resulting guilt. Let's look at it.

God's Standard of Perfection

God's system of handling guilt is fantastic. It works. Of course, the prerequisite to His system is that a person must have been justified by receiving Christ. Otherwise the system doesn't work. But here it is:

Accept. As we've seen so far, guilt is designed to be a useful factor in our lifestyles. It makes us *do* something about sin. The first step in handling guilt is to accept the fact that real guilt is not evil but is a good signal that something's wrong. Guilt motivates us to understand our behavior. It prods us toward correction of that behavior. So we don't need to be afraid of guilt feelings; we can accept them as a useful part of our everyday Christian lifestyle. Think of guilt as the "sorrow that is according to the will of God" of this verse:

> For the sorrow that is according to the will of God produces a repentance without regret, leading to salvation; but the sorrow of the world produces death (2 Corinthians 7:10).

Guilt is worthwhile! It points out a moral problem just as pain points out a physical problem. Without guilt we'd never do anything about sin!

Examine. "Test yourselves to see if you are in the faith; examine yourselves!" (2 Corinthians 13:5) When you feel a tinge of guilt, don't minimize or ignore it. Instead, examine it. Christians need to figure out what the guilt is signaling: What was wrong in what I did? What would be a better way to—under the Spirit's control—behave the next time that situation comes up? What does God's Word say about my action?

Not only does this quick self-exam pinpoint the wrongness of the act, but it's also a way to reveal any false guilt. Remember the little scenario at the beginning of the chapter about Stan whose parents were getting a divorce? Stan felt guilty about the divorce, as if *he* had caused the problem. Then his Christian "buddy" Arnie dumped more guilt feelings on him by saying he shouldn't be upset about the situation. If Stan followed God's plan on how to deal with guilt, he'd first accept the fact that he sure felt guilty and it probably meant something.

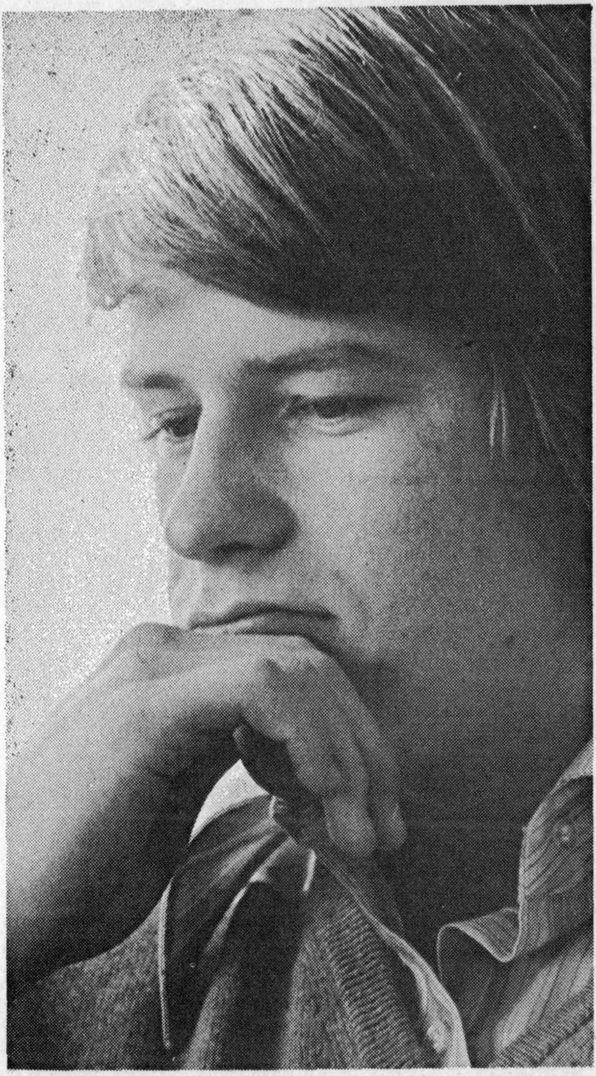

Next he'd examine his guilt feelings according to the Bible. And at this stage he would discover in Bible study and self-examination that he's not responsible for the decisions other people make (Romans 14:12) and that it's OK to feel upset (2 Corinthians 1:8). Then at least he could face his problems with a clear conscience.

False guilt can be inherited—maybe your parents feel guilty about so many things that you begin to feel guilty too, though you can't pin down what you've done. False guilt can be borrowed—someone has done something wrong and *you* end up feeling guilty (such as an illegitimate child feeling guilty when he's done nothing to deserve guilt). Fake guilt is dangerous—it can easily become neurotic guilt that rules a believer's life. You figure out whether you're feeling false guilt or the real thing by gauging your feelings by the Word of God.

If you think through an incident that made you feel guilty and God says specifically that activity is all right, then you've experienced a surge of false guilt. It wasn't really wrong. So thank God for the wisdom you've gained through that false guilt! If you aren't sure *what* the Bible teaches about the situation, get some help from your pastor or from a mature student of the Word. (My incredible book, *Anybody Here Know Right from Wrong?*, another SonPower Elective in this series, deals with this subject—how to know if something is really wrong or right.) If your self-examination, guided in Bible study, reveals that the activity *was* wrong, then you're set for the next step of God's plan for guilt.

Confess. Here it is, folks. The key to handling real guilt: "If we confess our sins, He is faithful and righteous to forgive us our sins and to cleanse us from all unrighteousness" (1 John 1:9).

Let's look at this verse in detail. "If we" points out two quick things about getting rid of guilt. First, the "we" refers only to Christians. A nonbeliever must first receive Christ before he can be included in this "we." Second, the "if" tells us that God's forgiveness is conditional. *If* we decide to confess, He will forgive. Christians can't go bombing through a lifestyle of sinning and not confessing, then expect to enjoy a clean fellowship with God. If not confessed, a Christian's sin and guilt *will* result in consequences—not in eternal death but consequences such as God's discipline (see 1 Corinthians 11:27-32; Galatians 6:7-8; Hebrews 12:5-11).

"To confess" doesn't mean to beg for forgiveness. A murderer's confession isn't an affair of "Please forgive me, guys. I didn't mean any harm when I pulled that trigger. How about forgiving me? Please?" No, it's more. "First I bought the gun at Freddy's gun shop; them I went to the apartment before the guy got home; then . . ." A confession describes what we did. Real confession says the same things as what really occurred—not, "God, forgive me for my sin," but "God, I did this; and then I did that; and this is how I feel aobut it; and this is the way I know You feel about it." Confession is saying the same thing that God would say about the whole incident. Confession makes us recognize and remember our sin.

"He is faithful and righteous" is a phrase that reminds us why God can forgive every sin we confess. When God forgives, He *faithfully* forgives! Even if we still feel guilty, God has forgiven the confessed sin. Still feeling the guilt reveals a false guilt, right? God is righteous, so He doesn't just pass over the sins. But in His righteousness, He knows that every one of those stinky little sins is paid for. The consequences were met long ago by Jesus Christ. The punishment that guilt demands has been handed out. We can instantly be declared "not guilty" because we've accepted Christ's prepayment!

"Forgiven and cleansed" is the state God puts us in as we confess. Forgiveness is a state, not necessarily a feeling. So when God forgives, we can know we've been awarded forgiveness, regardless of how we feel afterward.

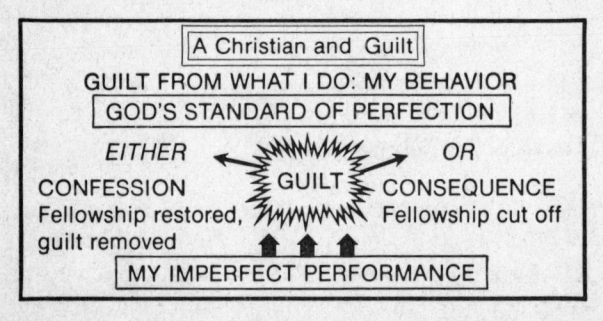

A Christian and Guilt

GUILT FROM WHAT I DO: MY BEHAVIOR

GOD'S STANDARD OF PERFECTION

EITHER ← GUILT → *OR*

CONFESSION — CONSEQUENCE
Fellowship restored, — Fellowship cut off
guilt removed

MY IMPERFECT PERFORMANCE

Correct. But of course God's program for guilt doesn't end there. He designed guilt to point out problem areas, remember? So now, in the guiltless freedom of our relationship and fellowship with God, we need to allow the Holy Spirit to correct the problem. The Word will define what the Spirit wants us to do. Maybe now we need to pay back a person we wronged. Maybe we need to straighten out a misunderstanding our actions caused. Whatever the lesson is, it'll be set down in black and white: "All Scripture is inspired by God and profitable for teaching, for reproof, for *correction,* for *training in righteousness*" (2 Timothy 3:16). The Word will give us the guidelines, and the Spirit will give us the power (Romans 8:4) to shape up our act in the future.

As we accept, examine, confess, and correct, we'll be handling our problems of guilt. God, the Judge of the universe, can daily pronounce us "not guilty."

Anger

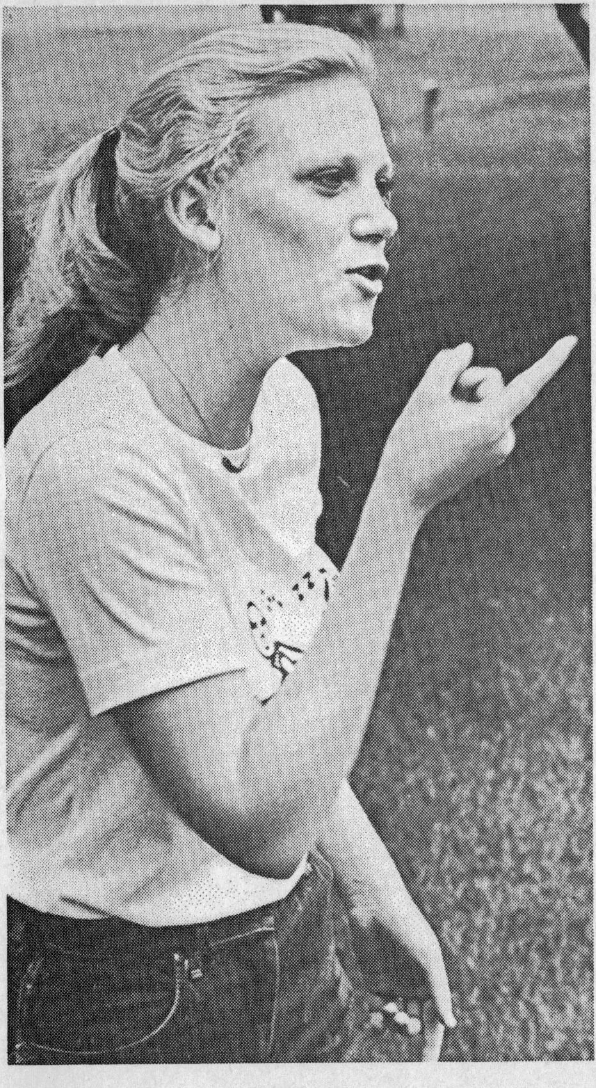

5
Don't Sizzle, Don't Explode

My pulse picks up first. My cheeks start to burn. Blood starts rushing through my body. My heart pounds. I seem to speed up all over. There's a sense of being keyed up and supercharged. I start to feel as if I'll burst or explode, as if there's too much inside to be held in, as if everything inside me is expanding, choking me.

I feel my fists clench. My senses are focused, my attention is riveted. There's an impulse to hurt, to hit, to kick someone, to strike out and smash or pound or bite. I want to say something that will hurt. I seem to be caught up, overwhelmed by the feeling. I'm completely wrapped up in the here and now—there's no thought of the past or future. I seem to be gripped by the situation.

I keep thinking about getting even, of revenge. I go over and over in my mind the cause of what I'm feeling. I keep searching for an explanation, for some understanding. There's a confused, mixed-up feeling, as though it almost feels good. I feel strong, tough.

I'm angry.

If you're somewhere between the ages of 10 seconds and 130 years, you know what it's like to be angry—to get mad. Maybe your anger is well controlled, expressed in quiet ways. Or maybe your anger is squelched inside, always kept to yourself. Or maybe you explode. But if you're basically human and have a nervous system, you'll get mad once in a while. Anger is one of those universal emotions, and it needs to be acknowledged and handled—acknowledged because it can be good, handled because it can be incredibly destructive.

Anger is not always bad or wrong. The Bible says, "Be angry"—go ahead and feel mad if you have to. But the rest of the verse says, "and yet do not sin"! (Ephesians 4:26). Anger can be expressed badly and wrongly—as you no doubt already know!

What Is It?

The word *anger* is associated with feelings of aggression, hostility, disgust, and contempt.

Anger is a strong feeling with strong physical symptoms. A little rundown of what happens in an angry body: The cerebral cortex chunk of the brain allows the hypothalamus to send little messages of

Don't Sizzle, Don't Explode / 109

"get mad!" through the autonomic nervous system. Then these impulses tell various glands to release all sorts of good stuff into the bloodstream. Next these secretions begin to affect different body parts—the heart speeds up; more blood is pumped out toward the muscles; there's a rise in blood sugar for extra strength; breathing increases; and pain sensors are dulled. The body gets mad.

But you don't have to memorize anatomical trivia in order to get your body into the anger act. It comes very naturally. The body in anger is preparing itself to overcome obstacles, to get ready for a fight. Anger provides physical strength. Have you ever noticed how powerful an angry person is? My skinny brother Tom had a wild knock-down-drag-out argument with our sister Beth over who could use the family car one night. After all kinds of verbal jabbing back and forth, Beth stomped into the bathroom and slammed the door. Meanwhile Tom's body, in his anger, transformed itself into—*Super Tom!* He grabbed a newspaper, rolled it tightly, and threw it at the door. It took my dad three days to patch the hole *through* the door and get it back straight on its hinges!

In primitive cultures, anger readies a person to protect himself. Getting mad when an 18-foot boa constrictor carries off his pet monkey is a natural part of the primitive man's survival. In our nice civilized societies, anger can provide confidence and emotional strength to overcome obstacles in the same way. Getting mad when some serpentine slob carries off your little sister's toy stuffed monkey is a

110 / From Rock Bottom to Mountaintop

natural part of modern man's lifestyle.

Anger is a physical and psychological reaction of displeasure. Let's look at a few illustrations.

Anger at things. I was in high school, riding in my cousin's "woody" from beach to beach around Monterey Bay in California. Cousin Joe was impressive in his Christian lifestyle—nearly a saint. But one afternoon as he chugged the woody up a ramp onto the freeway, Joe got angry at the car. It would not go fast. Two mammoth semi-trucks were bearing down on us rapidly from behind; and Joe yelled, "#%*#&*%' car!" I covered my ears.

You can be prodded into anger against things, as was the guy who blasted a hole through his TV screen with a shotgun because little lines kept going blip blip across it. You can get mad at stoplights that seem to know you're in a hurry. You can be mad at the wind that blew your English essay papers over approximately four square blocks. You can get angry at a thing.

Anger at people. Aren't parents wonderful stimuli for anger? Joel had made a deal with his dad that the yard work would be done before he would leave on a backpacking trip. Joel apparently missed the yard work; and when Dad insisted he couldn't go, Joel got mad. Joel's dad got mad. Long after the backpacking season, they were both still mad—at each other.

Helen and Sherry were best friends. Helen was dating a guy named Clark till Clark quit dating Helen in order to start dating Sherry. Helen was furious for months.

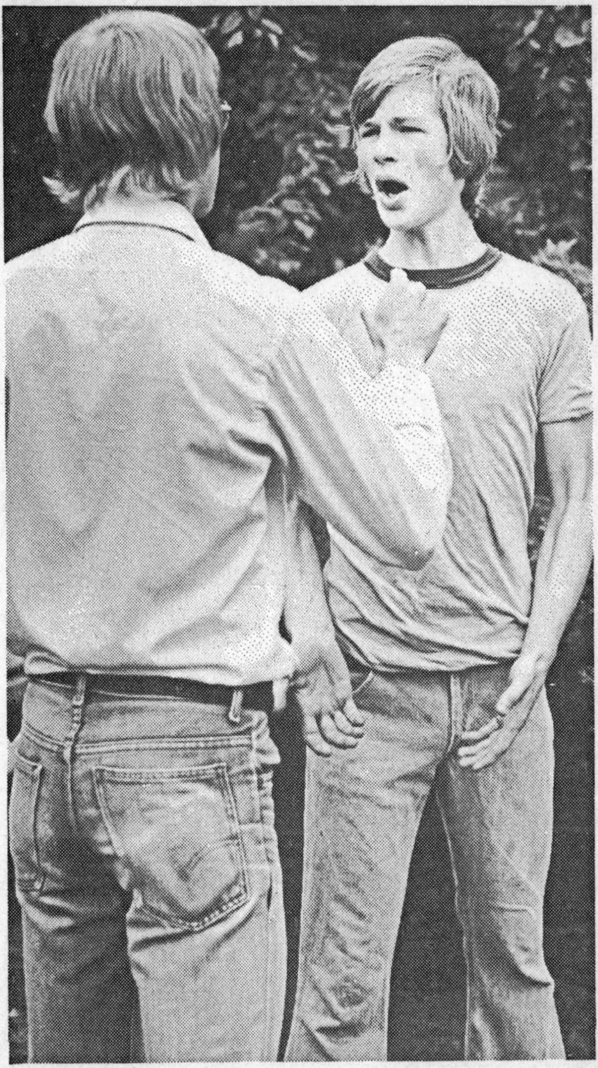

I was sitting on a stone porch overlooking a *barrio* street in Mexico when I noticed a mob of kids surrounding a boxing match between two boys. One of the little kids at the edge of the crowd had his head shaved—probably from a disease—and the other kids slapped and hit his bald head. I began to feel anger. After a while the crowd pushed the bald kid into the middle of the circle, forced the boxing gloves on him, and matched him up to fight a boy about two feet taller. And I got mad.

Once Jesus prepared to heal a man's shriveled hand on the Sabbath. His enemies surrounded Him to try to trap Him into a mistake so they could arrest Him. "Then Jesus asked them, 'Which is lawful on the Sabbath: to do good or to do evil, to save life or to kill?' But they remained silent. He looked around at them in anger and, deeply distressed at their stubborn hearts, said to the man, 'Stretch out your hand.' He stretched it out, and his hand was completely restored" (Mark 3:4-5, NIV). Jesus got angry! You can get angry at people.

Anger at self. I played soccer in college with a guy named Jim. He was a good soccer player, but like anybody, would miss a shot on the goal every once in a while. When he did—even in practice—Jim would leap in the air with a growl, fall down on his hands and knees, and thump his head on the ground in anger. Once after a missed shot, he kicked a post so hard he nearly broke his foot. He got mad at himself.

You can get mad at yourself for being such a klutz at athletics. You can get angry with yourself for for-

Don't Sizzle, Don't Explode / 113

getting your wallet in Terry's mother's car when Terry's mother just left on a cross-country trip. You can get mad at yourself for things that aren't worth getting angry over at all.

Anger at God. People can get angry at God. Some Christians get angry at God because they know He's there and He could do something about a problem if He just *would*. The Old Testament prophet Habakkuk seemed to get a little unsaintly at God: "Lord, I'm screaming and You *still* won't hear me! I shout HELP! VIOLENCE! and You *still* won't help me." (Read Habakkuk 1:2.)

You can look in the mirror and get angry at God for making you with too big a nose or too fat a head or too bugeyed. You *can* get mad at God.

How Don't I Deal with It?

Anger isn't an evil emotion. It's OK to be angry. But what isn't OK is wrong management of anger. The key question in handling anger is: How do I usually react when I'm angry? Do I say dumb things? Do I react with violence? Do I tighten up inside and do nothing externally?

Pushing it down inside. One of the dumbest concepts current among Christians is that never getting mad is a big sign of spirituality.

I was walking up to a house to visit an elderly lady one time, but a herd of neighborhood boys arrived at the door first. They presented the lady with a demolished bird house which they said they had accidentally smashed while climbing a tree in her yard. The lady's eyes glazed over; she squinted; she turned prune purple; she gripped the ex-bird house with whitening knuckles. Then she saw me, the visiting clergy-youth pastor. She cranked a grin at the kids, choking out, "That's all right, boys." Then she turned to me and said "Well, we all have our crosses to bear, don't we?" During the next half hour she never mentioned a word about the bird house but spoke sweetly about the Lord with her prune purple cheeks. She squelched her anger because she thought it wasn't spiritual to express it. She pushed it down inside.

Psychologists have proven that failure to respond to anger can cloud up your thinking, foul your ability to relate easily to others, and cause bodily problems from nervousness to hives to ulcers. Anger at God, if pushed down inside, can result in serious spiritual problems such as no desire for prayer (how can you confide in someone you're "secretly" mad at?), lack of trust, and bitterness.

Anger is such a powerful force that it's tough to stop it once it's off and running. If you try to squelch it, it seems to spurt out in another direction. My brother-in-law Doug is a little wiser now, but when he was four years old he jerked a hotel hallway fire hose down from its rack and the thing suddenly shot water like a geyser. Doug tried to hold the nozzle, but it whipped him slap-bang, swishing around the hallway. Doug's dad grabbed on and tried to hold his hand over the gusher, but it just sprayed out around his hand. The hotel was advertising second-

Don't Sizzle, Don't Explode / 115

floor canoe trips by the time the thing was finally turned off.

Anger is like that. If you try to push it down inside—"I am *not* going to be angry—I'm *not* going to let them know how mad I'm getting!"—anger will reveal itself in other spiritual, emotional and/or physical ways: in lack of faith, irritability, prayer problems, bitterness, not being able to concentrate, sleeplessness, nervousness, high blood pressure, and even complexion problems.

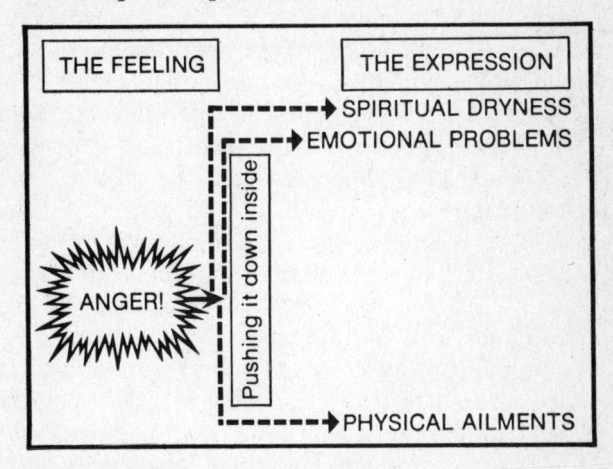

```
┌──────────────────────────────────────────────────┐
│  ┌─────────────┐           ┌─────────────────┐   │
│  │ THE FEELING │           │ THE EXPRESSION  │   │
│  └─────────────┘           └─────────────────┘   │
│                    ┌─────┐ ──→ SPIRITUAL DRYNESS │
│                    │     │ ──→ EMOTIONAL PROBLEMS│
│                    │Pushing                      │
│   ANGER!           │it down                      │
│                    │inside                       │
│                    │     │                       │
│                    └─────┘ ──→ PHYSICAL AILMENTS │
└──────────────────────────────────────────────────┘
```

Pushing anger down inside also can lead to depression. If a person constantly works at refusing to express anger, his emotional energy will be used up—just as it takes a lot of physical energy to bottle up the pressure of a fire hose. While that person's emotional strength is wasted on squelching any expression of anger, he has no emotional energy left to enjoy other feelings. He hardly feels anything at all—he's depressed.

Is it "spiritual" to push anger down inside and always be unruffled? No. To be spiritual is to be controlled by the Spirit of God. And to be spiritually mature is to become more like Jesus. And God, friends and neighbors, gets mad (Exodus 22:24). He expresses anger (Romans 3:5; Revelation 6:16; and other places). Many preachers hesitate to speak of God's wrath because they seem to think that anger isn't nice, isn't polite, isn't good. Consequently all nice, polite, good Christians aren't supposed to get mad, right? Wrong. Anger is a God-given, powerful emotion that's designed to be expressed in the right way. Squelching anger isn't "spiritual."

So don't push anger down inside. But don't just react either!

Letting it all out. One of the worst things you can do in boxing is lose your temper. Sure, a direct reaction to anger puts more power in your punch, but it also distorts your execution of the right techniques. Just ask a guy named Jerry from Redwood City, Calif. who enjoyed beating me to a pulp in Army boot camp. I lost my temper and obviously lost the boxing match. The natural reaction to anger is to hurt, to overpower, to win. And the natural reaction of anger is also to lose your head. This direct reaction of anger is sometimes called *venting*, and it's exactly that—giving vent to everything exactly as you feel it. This is another destructive way to handle anger. You feel like kicking your brother, and you kick your brother. You feel like screaming,

Don't Sizzle, Don't Explode / 117

"I hate you!" and you scream it. You feel like insulting your teacher, and without thinking you shout out anything that will hurt and humiliate. Letting-it-all-out works like this:

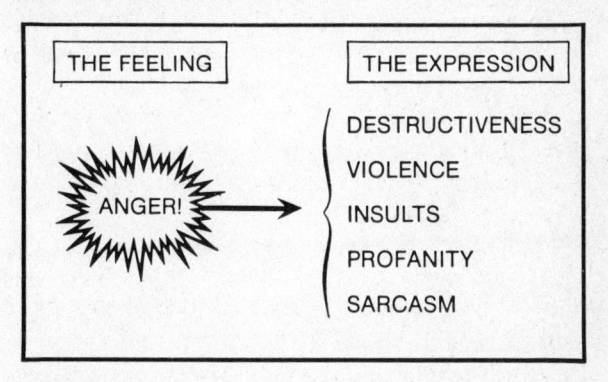

```
┌─────────────────────────────────────────────────┐
│   THE FEELING              THE EXPRESSION       │
│                                                 │
│                          ⎧ DESTRUCTIVENESS      │
│     ╱╲╱╲╱╲╱╲             ⎪                      │
│    ⟨  ANGER! ⟩────→      ⎨ VIOLENCE             │
│     ╲╱╲╱╲╱╲╱             ⎪ INSULTS              │
│                          ⎪ PROFANITY            │
│                          ⎩ SARCASM              │
└─────────────────────────────────────────────────┘
```

Identify with the process? Two cousins were arguing over which channel to watch on TV. One of the guys got so ticked off he ran to his bedroom, grabbed his rifle, and blew the other guy away. In the Old Testament King Saul got so angry at David that he threw his spear at him while David was trying to soothe Saul with harp music (1 Samuel 19:9-10). A soldier named Gentry was so angered when a Vietnamese peasant refused to answer questions that he slaughtered the man's entire family and burned his home before anyone could restrain him. A high school kid got so mad at himself after missing a field goal attempt in a championship football game that he went home, stuck a shotgun in his mouth, and pulled the trigger.

But don't leave the letting-it-all-out response to

anger at an illustration level. Think of some anger experiences you've had. Did you react in any of those situations with a let-it-fly expression of anger? Did you lose your temper? Do you ever say things when you're mad that you regret later—such as "I hate you!" or "I wish you were dead!" or other sweet things? Have you done something destructive as you acted out your anger—like breaking something, hitting someone, running away? If you're human, you probably have reacted in one of those ways.

An immediate reaction to anger is dangerous. Jesus said that if a person expresses anger he's on dangerous ground—he's in danger of judgment (Matthew 5:22) because the power of anger can easily be expressed in the wrong way.

But fortunately we're not just evolutionary machines that *have* to react in a cause-and-effect pattern: You made me mad so I'm going to make you mad! God offers help in this question of how to express anger in the right ways.

How Do I Deal with It?

All right? So everybody gets angry. And the wrong ways to handle the thing are to either squelch it inside or to blurt it all out. Now, what's the right way to get mad?

Decide now to quit being angry in the old-nature style. Right now, when hopefully you're not sizzling in the middle of an angry situation, decide that you don't want to handle your anger in the wrong ways. Expressions of anger which are based on our old sin nature won't work. The Bible repeatedly says to quit being angry the usual human way:

"Cease from anger, and forsake wrath" (Psalm 37:8).

"An angry man stirs up strife, and a hot-tempered man abounds in transgression" (Proverbs 29:22).

"Never take your own revenge" (Romans 12:19).

"Let all bitterness and wrath and anger . . . be put away from you" (Ephesians 4:31).

The old sin nature which is a part of every person has one way of getting mad—the wrong way; but the new nature in every Christian allows us to handle anger in the right way—in self-control.

Use restraint in your anger. Remember the anger process that the human body goes through? With the cerebral cortex and the hypothalamus and stuff? Well, believe it or not, every normal body's physical reaction to anger is about the same. The differences in what we call people's tempers come as people *handle* anger differently. That is, one kid allows himself to throw a gigantic tantrum and scream and drool when he experiences the same amount of anger as the guy who turns red and says, "I really get ticked off when you do that!" Regardless of your red hair or Irish blood or hot-tempered ancestors, you as a Christian *can* use restraint in expressing your anger. You can get to the biblical ideal of being "slow to anger":

"He who is slow to anger has great understanding" (Proverbs 14:29).

"A gentle answer turns away wrath" (15:1).

"The heart of the righteous ponders how to answer" (15:28).

"He who is slow to anger is better than the mighty" (16:32).

"Do not be eager in your heart to be angry" (Ecclesiastes 7:9).

"Let everyone be quick to hear, slow to speak, and slow to anger" (James 1:19).

Get the idea? The way to express anger is with a sense of restraint. And where do you get the restraint when the old temper starts to boil? From God, of course. If, as a Christian, you're being controlled by the Spirit, you *will* have self-control. It's a fruit of the Spirit, listed in Galatians 5:22-23. In other words, quit making excuses for yourself if you display a wild temper—as if you have no other choice. You can get angry and still maintain self-control as a Spirit-controlled believer.

Next, express your anger. With the Spirit's self-control, express how you feel. Notice that you don't express how you think the *other* person feels—"You always try to make me mad"; "You're just trying to hurt me." Tell the one you're mad at just how *you* feel. If it's another person, talk with him about it. If it's God you're angry with, tell Him about it. Express your feeling of anger:

"He who rebukes a man will afterward find more favor" (Proverbs 28:23).

"Be on your guard! If your brother sins, rebuke him" (Luke 17:3).

"Be angry, and yet do not sin; do not let the sun

go down on your anger, and do not give the devil an opportunity" (Ephesians 4:26-27).

In other words, do something about your anger. Don't just sit on it. Don't let a day go by without *expressing* how you feel about the situation.

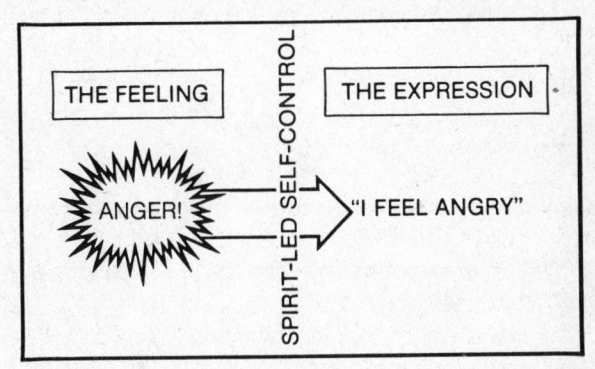

```
┌─────────────────────────────────────────────┐
│                      ┃                      │
│                      ┃                      │
│   ┌────────────┐     ┃   ┌──────────────┐   │
│   │ THE FEELING│  SELF-CONTROL │ THE EXPRESSION│  │
│   └────────────┘     ┃   └──────────────┘   │
│      ANGER!    ──SPIRIT-LED──▶ "I FEEL ANGRY" │
│                      ┃                      │
└─────────────────────────────────────────────┘
```

If a person has stimulated your anger, go to that person and talk face to face. Psychologists have found that "distance"—either a length of time or refusing to meet the person nose to nose—makes anger hotter because the offender becomes an impersonal opponent rather than a flesh-and-blood person. As you talk about your anger, take responsibility for your own feelings. Realize that it is you—not the other person or the situation—that allowed yourself to get mad. The problem may have been caused by that person or situation, but *you* are the source of the anger you're feeling.

Let's try to visualize this kind of restrained expression of anger as our heroine Diane handles her feelings about her brother Ken leaving for a party without her because she took so long getting ready: Diane sat on the couch and rummaged through her mind on how to get out of this mess. She checked the mirror again and wondered whether her flaming cheeks needed less blush-on now. When she decided that Kenny had had enough time to get to the party, she dialed with a still-shaky finger. "Rod? Hi. Is Kenny there yet? Let me talk to him, OK?"

"Hello?"

"Kenny," her voice started to shake and she instantly prayed for some Spirit control. "Kenny, I feel so mad I hardly know what to do. . . ."

"Well, it's your fault!" Ken wasn't exactly unruffled himself.

"I know it's my fault; but I wish you wouldn't have taken off without me. I'm mad because I'm left here at home, you know? I feel so left out. . . ."

"Yeah, I hear you. I'll drive over and get you."

"I'm still mad."

"That's OK. I guess you need to be at the party—mad or not, huh?"

"Thanks, Kenny. 'Bye." Diane's anger seemed to fall off her shoulders now as she hurried to repolish the finishing touches on her makeup. By the time Kenny bleeped the horn she was ready, more intent on who would be at the party than on being mad at Ken.

Sound dumb? Like a Christian soap opera? Face it, when things work out the right way we don't think it's a good story. But it does illustrate the prin-

Don't Sizzle, Don't Explode / 123

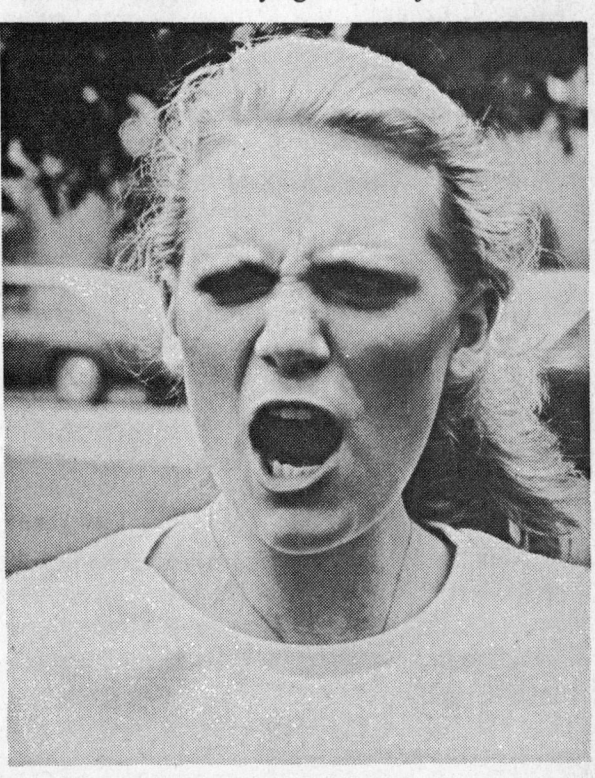

ciple of handling anger with restrained expression. Diane *was* angry—why deny it? She prayed for Spirit control as she sought to talk about it with her brother as quickly as possible. And she expressed her own feelings—she didn't start the phone conversation with "You stupid idiot, you stink, you know that?" If she had, she'd still be sitting at home, right? Instead she worked at saying how *she felt:* "I feel so mad—I'm mad because I'm left here at home—I feel so left out."

When you encounter your own anger in a situation, express with restraint what you're feeling by using "I feel" language. Don't babble about "You did this" and "You did that." Start by actually saying, "I feel . . ." *Afterward, work at problem solving.* Once you've cooled down, begin to figure out the value of your anger experience. It can point out an area where you have a problem. With Diane and Ken, the incident pointed out a problem of simple scheduling. They'll need to sit down when both are thinking straight and draw up a contract as to when Diane needs to be ready if Ken is driving her somewhere. Your screeching session with your mother maybe pointed out a problem in your television-watching habits. Work it out, talk about a plan that will avoid future temper-igniting scenes. When you're no longer angry because you expressed your feelings with self-control, sit down and answer two questions about your anger-inciting incident:

1. What, specifically, is the conflict?
2. What are some possible solutions to the conflict?

If you got angry at your parents because they wouldn't let you go skiing over the weekend—the conflict may be about how much activity you think you should enjoy. A solution might be to schedule a calendar, to specify in advance how many nights you can expect to go somewhere.

If you got angry at God because He allowed your application to your favorite college to be rejected—

maybe the conflict is in your realizing who knows your future the best. A solution would be studying exactly how to determine God's will for your life.

So anger can be a stepping stone to better relationships, a more disciplined life, a deeper understanding of God's universe.

This Is It, Folks

Anger itself isn't bad. It's what you do with it that counts. And the keys to handling anger include expressing your feelings with Spirit-led restraint, then afterward working toward a solution of the anger-inciting conflict.

You'll notice we didn't talk much about "righteous indignation." That's a phrase people sometimes use to justify their rash expressions of anger. It's OK to be righteously indignant, to be ticked off at sin; but angrily slitting somebody's throat because he's wrong *is* wrong. Anger at injustice, immorality, or corruption—as when Jesus raised havoc with the temple money changers—still needs to be expressed in self-control. The controlled-anger principle applies whether you're angry for a momentous, noble cause or because mother washed your white T-shirt with your jeans. We also didn't talk about wild, exaggerated anger as a chronic problem. That's because that kind of anger—habitual, out-of-control rage—means it's time to seek professional help from a Christian psychiatrist, counselor, or pastor.

Depression

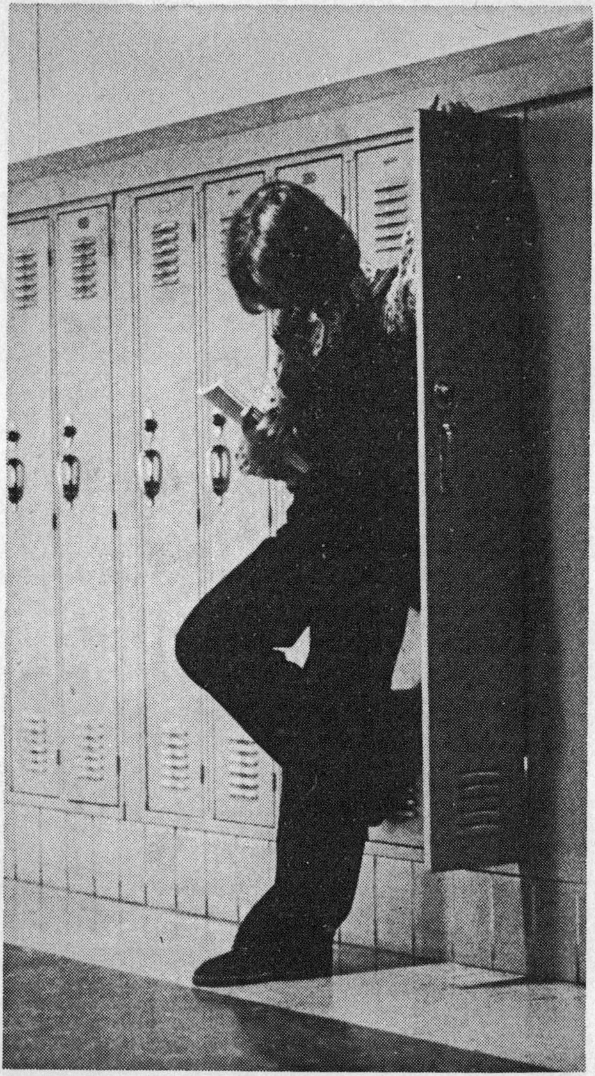

6
Don't Bug Me Today

Cindy walked toward the bus stop, feeling her feet burn on the hot sidewalk. Her arm was awkwardly cramped with half a dozen textbooks. She stuck her purse between her teeth as she struggled to keep the books from falling. Then she stopped and her notebook fell to the concrete. Her eyes shut, she slowly loosened her grip, letting the other books drop with a thump. She opened her eyes and stared at the mess.

Her bus hissed as it pulled up to the curb just as she picked up the last of her books. "Hey, Cindy, you forgot that envelope," said someone on the bus, pointing to a brown envelope on the sidewalk.

She ignored the comment and walked back to her seat.

When she staggered in the front door, her sister said, "Hi, Cindy. How'd it go today?" She frowned at the smug, complacent look on her sister's face as she sat knitting.

"Shut up," Cindy said.

"Get your report card today?"

Cindy pretended to not hear the question as she pushed the door into the kitchen open. "Mom, I've got to talk—"

Glancing up from her nails she was carefully polishing, her mother said, "Cynthia, you're all sweaty. You go right upstairs and take a shower."

"Get your report card?" she heard again from her sister as she trudged upstairs. She turned on the radio and waited for what she knew was coming.

A half hour passed since she turned up the volume and tried to shut out of her mind the droning song lyrics and everything else.

Her dad's voice broke through the noise.

"Cindy! I want to see those grades!"

"Sure, Dad." She sat in front of the mirror and stared unblinking at herself, seeing nothing. Like last week, she knew she couldn't cry.

What? Me Depressed?

Ever get depressed? Everybody does at one time or another. Over a million and a half people in the United States alone are currently undergoing treatment for severe depression, and experts claim that up to 15 million *should* be getting professional treatment. Depression is common, and one of its sourest periods during a life span occurs during youth.

I'm Depressed, but I Don't Feel Anything

Sometimes people describe depression as nothing more than a bad feeling. Nothing ever goes right.

But if you want to get picky, depression isn't really a feeling—it's a *lack* of feeling. Let me explain. A real feeling, an emotion, is a *response* to someone or something. You get slaughtered in Ping-Pong, you feel angry and you yell, "Stupid game!"—or worse. Somebody you really care about says, "I just don't like being around you anymore" and you *feel* hurt in response.

Depression isn't a response either, such as not being able to cry when you need to. Loneliness is a feeling, a response; but it can be pushed down out of sight because you don't want to feel it. If you box up a feeling such as loneliness, a lot of other feelings are boxed up and squelched too. Pretty soon you don't feel anything at all. And you're depressed.

But before we start shrewdly psychoanalyzing each other, let's look at a list of what happens when a person is depressed. Maybe that'll help clarify just what the monster is.

Depression Isn't Fun

Some symptoms of depression are:
1. Not being able to enjoy even good things
2. A lack of concentration, indecision
3. Feeling physically tired, lack of energy

4. Irritability—you're crabby and you know it
5. Not being able to sleep well
6. Suicidal thoughts
7. Physical aches, cramps
8. Unusual urges—thinking drastic things (such as harming a friend)

And if we were official "shrinks" in analyzing depression, the list could go on for pages.

Just remember this: Depression can get to be a serious, prolonged condition. Don't always try to play psychiatrist on yourself—when depression is extended and severe, professional counseling is the only way to go.

Causes of Depression

Along with unbelievable homework assignments, three things can drive you into a nagging depression: problems, stress, and unrealistic goals. In your youth, you're surrounded by all three.

Problems. Whether they're ugly situations that pop up occasionally (wrecking your parents' car, flunking a quiz, getting zits), or whether they're permanent hassles (one of your legs is shorter than the other, you may be too short—or too tall), problems often lead to depression.

Stress. Stress is generally the amount of pressure that squeezes you when a major change or crisis catches up with you. Moving to a new area with a new school and new people is a giant stress factor which, unless dealt with, can drown you in depression. Have you ever gone through the trauma of a family divorce, having someone you love die, or being fired from a job or flunking in school? Depression can chew you up after such stressful incidents.

Unrealistic goals. This might be a tough one to understand as a possible source of depression. The basic needs or goals of any human being are to love and to be loved and to feel worthwhile.

Let's say Jake Kale sets a goal of buying a Corvette and having $5,000 in savings when he's 18. From the time he's 9 years old, Jake kills himself to save money from his two after-school jobs. He works like an idiot every summer and every vacation. So he finally reaches his 18th birthday, goes out and buys his Corvette, checks to see that he's got his $5,000 in savings, and after his birthday party gets wildly depressed. Why? Jake probably figured he'd really be worth something by being "successful." But reaching his made-up goals hasn't really met his *basic* needs. And he's depressed.

Unrealistic goals such as I'll-really-be-something-when-I-graduate or I'll-be-popular-when-I-can-buy-better-clothes are bound to drag you into depression once you've either failed at the goal or reached it, still feeling unloved and worthless. Maybe you've been to a Christian summer camp where you made a dazzling commitment to the Lord ("I'm going to talk to every kid at school about Christ!") only to fail miserably and feel depressed three weeks later.

Why Do I Get Depressed?

If you want to stay away from depression altogether you should acknowledge the feelings you have—don't try to coolly cover up or ignore even painful feelings.

There's an exercise to help you understand your feelings and what you're doing about them right now. Think through the following diagram. If you can, supply some examples of what happens to you in the column on the right.

| CAUSE (problem, stress, or unrealistic goal) | Clancey's family moves to a new own. Clancey finds himself with few friends, and blames his parents for forcing him to leave old friends back home. | A hassle that gets me down: |

FEELING	If Clancey would think about his feeling, he feels angry about the move. He feels it's unfair.	How I feel about my problem:
REPRESS THE FEELING	Clancey won't talk about how he feels about the move. In fact, Clancey hardly talks at all anymore —to anyone.	How I avoid or cover up my feeling:
DEPRESSION	Trying to cover up or suppress his anger, Clancey makes no friends, doesn't talk to his parents unless they ask him something, and spends hours and hours watching TV. Clancey's depressed.	How I act when I'm depressed:

Get the idea? Depression tackles you when you refuse to acknowledge or handle some painful feelings. You—even subconsciously—decide *not* to feel.

If you're like me, when you skimmed over the diagram you didn't really think through a personal incident of depression. But take a pencil and do it now for a few valuable minutes. You can afford to slow down your breathless reading of the thrilling conclusion of this chapter to do something really important:

• Pick a sour depression-time you experienced,

at a time when you were really down. Maybe even now?

- Write out the cause that first got you into the mess. Was it a problem? Stress? Failing at unrealistic goals?
- Really think through the type of feeling which would be a natural response to the cause. Anger? Fear? Frustration? Humiliation? Guilt? Identify the feeling as if it were somebody else's problem.
- If you didn't deal with the feeling, you suppressed your feelings and you became depressed. Do you see now *why* you got depressed? Write out how you acted, what you did.

Now let's figure out just what to do once you *are* down.

How Do I Deal with Depression?

Regardless of how bad things are, you should deal with feelings that may be painful—but you don't have to get depressed. Here are four steps to follow in dealing constructively with painful feelings:

Step 1 Make sure you've been born again. If you're going to tackle a demon such as depression, you'll need God's presence in you. And you need to be sure of God's presence. Read over that chapter on guilt for details on how you can be certain Christ is in you.

Step 2 Determine how you really feel about the situation. You may have been depressed for so long that you don't even know when you're angry or frustrated. Dr. Tim LaHaye, in *How To Win Over Depression,* says, "Most depressed persons cannot and do not think of themselves as angry people." So you might need some help in figuring out what you'd really be feeling if you weren't mushed down in depressive *un*feeling. And the "help" will come in handy for the next step:

Step 3 Express the way you feel. Alexander Lowen, in his book *Depression and the Body,* writes, "The person who can openly express his dependent needs is not as likely to become depressed as the person who hides them behind an appearance of independence." Tell yourself out loud how you feel about the situation. Write about it. Pray about it.

Prayer is a fantastic tool for expressing how you feel about a problem. David's Psalms are a good example of how to express prayers to God. Read through Psalms 13; 22; 38 ("there is no soundness in my flesh . . . neither rest in my bones . . . I am troubled . . . I am feeble . . . my strength fails me . . . my friends stand aloof") or Psalm 42 ("O my God, my soul is cast down within me"). David knew how to express what he felt to God in prayer. But watch it—continued self-pitying prayer will get you nowhere unless you move to Step 4.

Talking, writing, phoning somebody is the next best expression to prayer. Your parents are prime candidates to talk to, but a lot of kids have hassles communicating with parents. If that's your situation, maybe a mature friend, a teacher, a Christian adult, a pen pal, a school counselor, or your pastor will listen to you. "A mirror reflects a man's face, but what he is really like is shown by the kind of friends he chooses" (Proverbs 27:19, LB).

Step 4 Deal with the Cause. This is the final, crucial step in salvaging yourself from depression. *Do* something about the original cause. If it was a problem, stress, or disappointment at an unrealistic goal, you've got to move into action. In what ways?

If possible, change the situation that's giving you the headaches.

Cindy, in the story at the beginning of this chapter, had several causes to tackle, but the only one she could try to *change* is the hassle of not being able to communicate with her parents. So Cindy started something that seemed dumb at first, but she wrote letters to her parents. And sensing her sincerity, her mother and father answered the letters with more letters. It almost got to be a joke, but they began to communicate. Cindy did something to change one of the causes of her depression and gained a new source of listeners when she needed to express her feelings.

Another way to deal with the cause is to change yourself. If you can't do a thing about improving a bad situation, then Steps 1-3, you can adjust. For example, Cindy was depressed about grades—let's assume she was doing the best she could.

After making sure of her relationship with Christ, after pinning down her feelings of anger because she felt the grading system unfair, and after expressing how she felt to her parents through letters—then Cindy can deal with the unchangeable cause (she *has* to go to school and work for grades). She

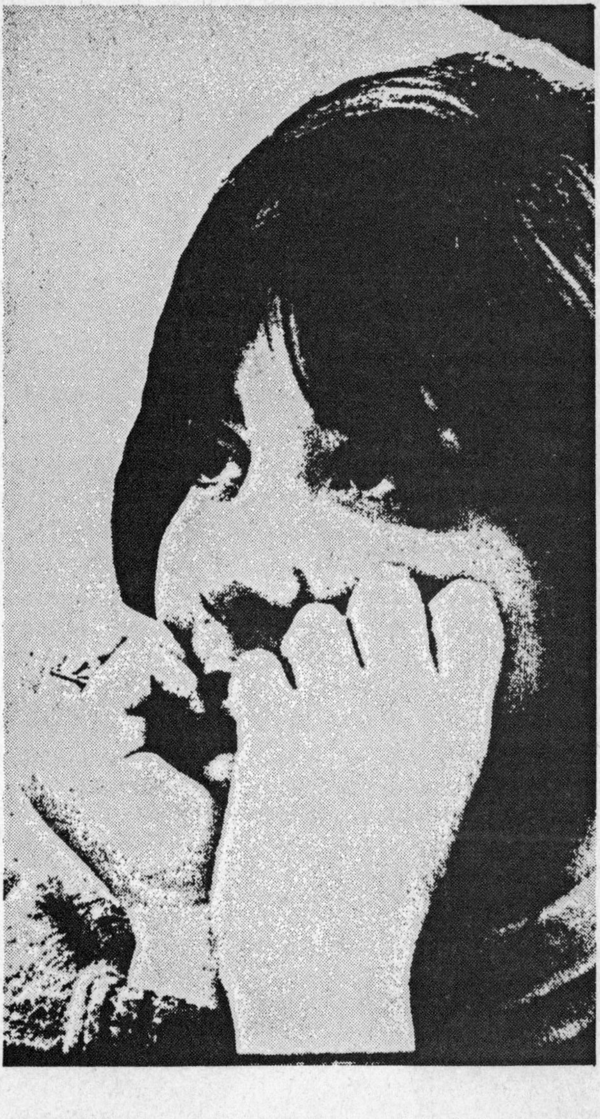

can change by catching the attitude that she's important, even if she's never able to get A's, by finding and developing herself in an activity where God has given her abilities (gymnastics? helping with children? a hobby?). Cindy doesn't have to stop trying in her schoolwork, but she can put some energy into something she'll enjoy. Cindy could decide to do things with other kids—even when she doesn't feel like it—and stifle the urge to let loneliness push her into depression.

The Apostle Paul had a physical problem which he couldn't change. Theologians guess that Paul's physical problems might have resulted from the dozens of times he was whipped and stomped on because of his stand for Christ.

But whatever the specific cause, Paul couldn't change it. "Three times I pleaded with the Lord to take it away from me. But He said to me, 'My grace is sufficient for you, for My power is made perfect in weakness'" (2 Corinthians 12:8-9, NIV). God was able to help Paul accept the unchangeable problem. So what was Paul's new attitude toward the hassle? "Therefore, I will boast all the more gladly about my weaknesses, so that Christ's power may rest on me" (2 Corinthians 12:9b, NIV).

God can give you the desire and ability to accept an unchangeable problem. He'll use it to change *you*.

Do you have any physical problems like Paul's? Maybe you have constant, agonizing hassles with what TV commercials call—ever so politely— "blemishes." They show some dazzling guy or girl with perfectly clear skin dabbing a squirt of gook on an invisible spot. Almost instantly the kid's love life is transformed, right? Maybe your blemishes aren't the commercial variety. And maybe your complexion affects the way you feel about relationships, meeting new people, going to big events (zits always seem to come bursting out just in time for a banquet, a big date, cheerleader tryouts, or school pictures!).

I had that kind of a hassle in high school, and I know it affected the way I felt about myself. I mean, how can you maintain a decent self-image when your best friends call you "Pizzaface"? And when none of the miracle remedies worked, I got depressed.

What could I do? First, I could make sure I was keeping a straight relationship with God. Secondly, I could identify my feelings of embarassment and anger every time I peeked in the mirror. Third, I could express my feelings to a friend or God—or both. ("But Lord, Irving Stenkies doesn't have zits and he isn't even a Christian!") And finally, since I couldn't change the situation, I needed to accept my complexion as a God-directed opportunity to concentrate on things other than my face. I could work on developing inner qualities such as faith or friendliness. I didn't win the "best-looking" category in the yearbook, but I found out how not to be depressed. And so the whole complexion hassle was worth it.

Joy!

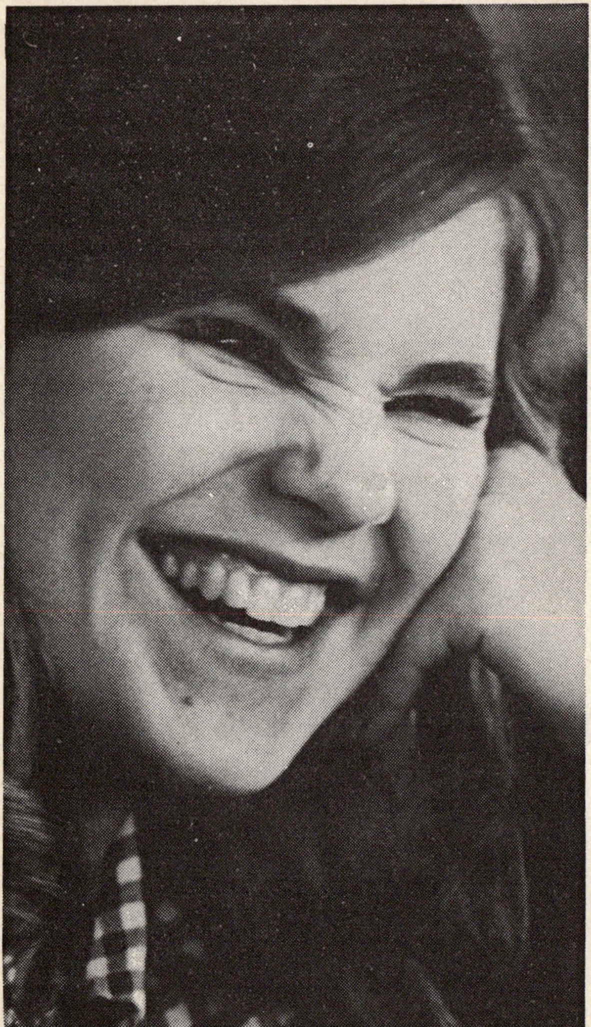

7
Catch Those Fantastic Feelings

The gut-wrenching smell of the shack forced me outside for air. I breathed the hot air heavily, then leaned in through the window to try to sing again: *"Allá en el cielo . . ."*

The old man blinked watery, blind eyes to the cadence. It was the only Spanish song I knew, so I sang it again as he blinked. He was lying grotesquely on the wooden platform. I swung at the flies again from the window, but now I was too far away to keep them from creeping under his bandages.

He didn't smile. Didn't speak. His skin hung rigid and dry across his face like plastic, and he didn't move even to readjust his shattered legs. I finished the song.

"Que Dios le bendiga." I said it like a child. "God bless you." Then I struggled over the rocks back

down the hill from the shack. I thought he would die soon. The church would mourn deeply.

* * *

Another year wound around, and I was back in Guaymas. The telegraph office steps were bare except for a single beggar who sang to himself. He didn't turn his head as I clicked up the stairs, but he smiled and held out his hat. I barely remembered the blind eyes, but winced as I recognized his song. I dug for *pesos*. *You're not supposed to know beggars,* I was thinking. If you knew them they shouldn't have to beg. I wondered if his legs had healed but I felt too confused to ask. I folded three *dólares* in the hat, stood awkwardly beside him, then felt disgusted with myself as I shuffled away without speaking.

* * *

The beetles buzzed in the darkness as I watched the church elders carry the same blind man to a seat along the aisle. He sang none of the hymns, sat through the prayers, eyes blinking slowly. I watched as he fumbled three *dólares* into the offering plate. Then when testimony time came, he grabbed the bench before him and rose to his feet. The congregation gasped.

"You see I stand," he began in Spanish. "As for myself, I cannot see that I stand, but I feel my legs growing strong again. So I bless the Lord among you, my precious brothers and sisters. For the Lord is good. He is great to be praised." He turned his eyes toward heaven as if he could see. "And the depths of my heart are full today, for the Lord is healing my legs, giving me joy. I exult in Him!" And he began to sing the song, "*Allá en el cielo*—there in heaven, there in heaven. There are no more tears, no more sadness, no more sorrow. . . ."

I had never seen such joy on a man's face. I had never seen such joy.

Such joy.

Can you be a joyful person like the old man? Make a mental list of the obstacles that are keeping you from a lifestyle stuffed with joy.

Think back over your list. Are the problems mostly circumstances like not having enough money? Not being physically healthy or strong or coordinated? Not being attractive? Ending up in the wrong family? Having a slow brain? Being bored? Living in a neighborhood that's definitely low-budget? Going to a hostile school? Feeling bad about losing somebody you love? Getting beaten up? Being born with a strange body?

Well, great! You can put a huge X over the whole list of reasons. Because regardless of who you are, regardless of the bad-news circumstances in your life, you can have joy! Joy doesn't come from the right circumstances, and joy doesn't come from having the "right" personality. Joy comes from God—and He's available to everybody regardless of race, color, national origin, or shoe size. He's ready to dispense an incredible quantity of joy to anybody—even you. The Bible says about God, "Thou wilt make known to me the path of life; in Thy presence is fullness of joy; in Thy right hand there are pleasures forever" (Psalm 16:11).

Tell Me about It

It's 8 A.M. You leap out of bed, terror-stricken because you overslept. You land on your dumb brother's skateboard left strategically next to the bed and careen screaming into the walk-in closet. You duck to avoid the shelf and bash your forehead across the clothes bar, fall backward out of the closet with a coat draped over your head, and singe your seat on the heater duct. You pound the floor in rage; and a big, dusty book falls off the desk, bonks you on the ear, and flops open to an underlined passage: "Rejoice evermore!"

So maybe you're not happy today. "How are you?" someone asks; and you say, "No fun." But as the little church-front sign reads: "Happiness depends on happenings; joy depends on Jesus!"

Joy is pretty tough to define. The old Apostle Peter said that when somebody's really into joy, he can't explain it; it's "joy inexpressible" (1 Peter 1:8). But everybody can identify with what it means to feel really good, right? You feel on top of things; your senses are sharp and clear. You feel eager; your sense of well-being makes you feel important, optimistic. You've got gusto, zest, enthusiasm!

You're ready to take on the whole world.

Basically, feeling really good happens in two ways: One, it happens as a result of external things. Or two, feeling good happens as a result of something internal. The external factor that can make you feel great is called *pleasure*. The internal factor is *joy*. Pleasure is great. But since the good feelings it brings depend on changeable circumstances (from the temperature to who sits next to you to how your morning eggs are cooked), pleasure comes and goes.

Joy, on the other hand, results in similar good feelings regardless of how things are going. Joy is a spiritual element that God puts *inside* you. It can have you feeling great even in the worst situations. Remember the biblical account of Paul and Silas in the Philippian jail? After being humiliated, dragged through the streets, stripped, beaten to a pulp, tossed into a dungeon, and stuck in stocks, Paul and Silas started singing (Acts 16:16-34). This is the same Paul who, beaten again and again in prison, wrote that because of this, "I rejoice, yes, and I will rejoice" (Philippians 1:18). Paul said this too: "I delight in weaknesses, in insults, in hardships, in persecutions, in difficulties. For when I am weak, then I am strong" (2 Corinthians 12:10). Get it? Paul was happy that things around him weren't so hot.

There's got to be something either very wrong or else very right about a guy like that. Because though Paul didn't have much going for him in terms of what was happening around him, he could still rejoice.

150 / From Rock Bottom to Mountaintop

Think through the value of real joy:

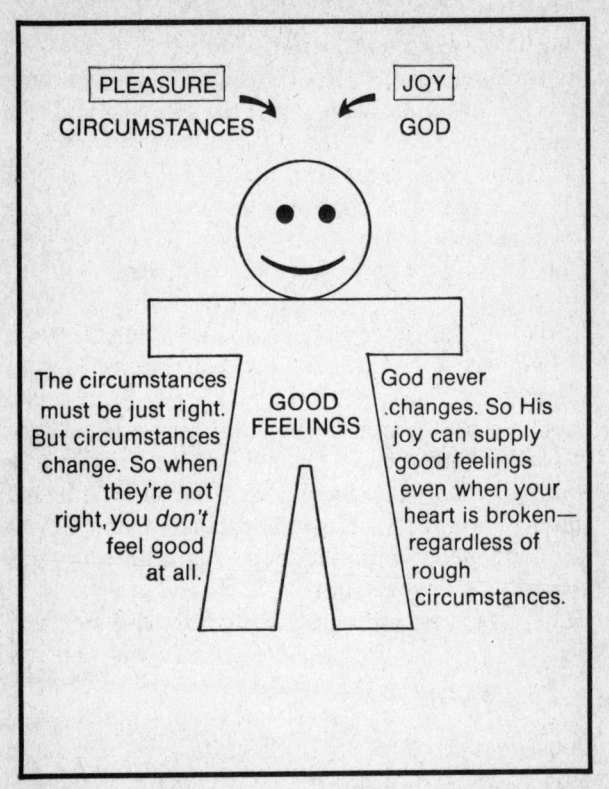

PLEASURE → ← JOY

CIRCUMSTANCES　　　　GOD

The circumstances must be just right. But circumstances change. So when they're not right, you *don't* feel good at all.

GOOD FEELINGS

God never changes. So His joy can supply good feelings even when your heart is broken—regardless of rough circumstances.

But you basically know all this so far, right? That joy is a valuable commodity. It's something more than good times and grins. And it makes sense that such a beautiful thing as joy would come from God. Now, how do you get ahold of it? How do you have joy?

How to Enjoy

Henry David Thoreau said, "The mass of men lead lives of quiet desperation." But it doesn't have to be that way. God can drench anyone—and everyone—with joy.

Are you familiar with the fruit of the Spirit? (Galatians 5:22-23) "The fruit of the Spirit is love, *joy,*" etc. Joy comes from God as a fruit of the Spirit. Now, how do you chomp into it?

Fruit dangling on a tree develops because the tree is alive. There aren't many petrified forests sprouting pomegranates. So the first key to enjoying joy is to make sure you have the life of the Spirit in you. If you've made a decision to trust Christ, the Holy Spirit made sure you were born again (see John 3:1-8), and He came into you (Romans 8:9) to give you life (8:11). If you're a born-again believer, you've got God's life in you—life that can produce fruit such as joy.

It takes time for a plant to show the world its fruit. Jack's giant beanstalk that grew overnight is just a fairy tale. And, in the same way, Christians don't grow spiritual fruit overnight. A believer has to spend *time* immersed in the energizing life of the Spirit before fruit appears. Now if that sounds either too mystical or too theological, stick with me. When the Spirit of God stepped into my body, I immediately began making choices as to whether I would let Him live through my body or whether the old me would take over the controls of my brain, mouth, hands, and eyeballs. The more I let my old self control my life, the more sick results came out of me. Or the more time I allow the Spirit to live His life through me, the more I develop the fruit of the Spirit.

The point is, don't expect dazzling balls of joy to light up your life if you're controlled by the Spirit for about two minutes every other week. As you know, even a Christian won't feel joy if he's not living a lifestyle that's characterized by Spirit control. If he's self-controlled most of the time, the only way he's going to feel good for a while is to go the pleasure/circumstances/kicks route that non-Christians are limited to. And there's no real joy there.

Joy comes when God the Spirit steps into your life, when you spend most of your time being controlled by Him. But let's be realistic—does ultimate joy automatically pop up inside you some morning after you've spent a special quota of hours walking in the Spirit? Not really. In nitty-gritty life, the Spirit will develop in you a growing sense of joy through two methods. He will direct you into some specific *habits* that uncover joy and into all kinds of *hassles* that will reveal this fruit of the Spirit.

Habits

The Holy Spirit will guide you into habits as you develop joy. Let's look at a few of these practices:

Obedience. "The execution of justice is joy for the righteous" (Proverbs 21:15). As you do the things

Catch Those Fantastic Feelings / 153

God wants you to, you'll be joyful. Jesus put it this way when speaking of His commandments: "These things I have spoken to you, that My joy may be in you, and that your joy may be made full" (John 15:11). Be sure to catch the right perspective on this. Just running out and doing your Official Good Deed for the day won't necessarily result in ecstatic joy. But, guided by the Spirit, accomplishing what God has stated in His Word will develop joy. The joy comes not because you're chalking up goody points with God to impress Him, but because doing the right thing is the best way to live.

For example: Glen and Sandie were growing in a rich relationship of love. Both of them sensed that God would bring them together for a lifetime. They talked about the practicalities of marriage quite a bit. The closer they grew in love, the more difficult it became to handle their physical pull toward each other. And yet it was an area where they used their brains. God commands that believers stay away from fornication. Glen and Sandie knew that the biblical word for fornication *(pornea)* doesn't just mean "going all the way"; it also refers to any sexual sin. So they determined that by the control of the Spirit they would obey. They sensed the Spirit's wisdom guiding them to mutually set some "ground rules": They would not lie down together, they would not remove clothing. . . . And what do you suppose the result was in their premarital relationship? In their eventual marriage? The result was joy! The concept and anticipation of how God had designed their sexual responses for marriage brought such a sense of joy into Glen and Sandie's relationship that now they never even think twice about the discipline it took to obey God's laws. And what heightened their joy before and after the wedding ceremony was the knowledge that their self-discipline in that area was absolutely the *best* thing they could do in a relationship. God knows what He's talking about.

Knowledge of the Word. Studying, meditating, memorizing, and understanding the Word of God is a Spirit-powered source of joy. The Bible hits over and over again the joy that the Word brings: "I have rejoiced in the way of Thy testimonies, as much as in all riches. . . . I shall delight in Thy statutes. . . . Thy testimonies are also my delight" (Psalm 119:14, 16, 24). Jeremiah said, "Thy words were found, and I ate them, and Thy words became for me a joy and the delight of my heart" (Jeremiah 15:16). A Spirit-controlled study of the Word will bring joy.

But (I can already hear what you're thinking as you read this)—what if you *tried* studying the Bible and it just seemed that it was drier than *you* were? What if you didn't feel any tingly sparks of joy after you studied?

Relax. You're experiencing what most Christians go through in their Bible study at one time or another. It's the "I studied/it didn't do anthing/how come?" question.

To answer the question we need to consider two things:

First, we often grind into the Bible on our own power, reading and studying because we think we're supposed to. What we need is to be Spirit-powered as we dig in. Last week I decided to meditate through a phrase that seemed empty of meaning the last time I tried to study Psalm 91. This time I asked God the Spirit to tear away the garbage in my life and to control my thinking as I studied. The phrase was, "Surely He shall deliver thee from the snare of the fowler" (91:3, KJV). Big deal, huh? But as God directed my thinking, I watched the goofy little phrase explode into a whole new revelation about God's dealing with me. I reeled with joy. A few buddies asked, "Hey, Stearns. What're you on?" And I grinned and said, "Psalm 91:3!"

The other problem in not experiencing joy through Bible study is that sometimes it doesn't blossom forth right when we study. Remember that joy is a Spirit-produced fruit and that it takes time to develop. So joy won't necessarily come bubbling out of your ears when you flip open the Book, murmur 11 words of print, and then fall asleep. Kids will often say, "I studied, but nothing happened." Fine. But something *will* happen in the long run if you become a Spirit-powered student of the Word. Your lifestyle will be different. *You* will be different. Joy will happen.

Witnessing. Sharing what Christ has done produces joy. John the Baptist compared himself to the best man at a wedding, while Christ was compared to the groom: "He who has the bride is the bridegroom; but the friend of the bridegroom, who stands and hears him, rejoices greatly because of the bridegroom's voice. And so this joy of mine has been made full" (John 3:29). John was a witness to Christ, as a best man is a witness at a wedding. And that privilege of witnessing about Christ brings joy. Another New Testament notable wrote to those he had introduced to the Lord, "For who is our hope or joy or crown of exultation? Is it not even you, in the presence of our Lord Jesus at His coming? For you are our glory and joy" (1 Thessalonians 2:19-20). Here the Apostle Paul says that helping others toward a born-again experience brings joy.

Etc. I could keep plowing through these Spirit-induced habits that bring joy: Meekness brings joy (Isaiah 29:19); asking and receiving in prayer brings joy (John 16:24); fellowship with other Christians brings joy (2 John 12), etc. But you already know that you're supposed to do all these things as a good Christian, right? You're supposed to obey, to study the Word, to witness, to be meek, etc. And you're thinking, "Oh, it's the same old stuff." Right! The same old stuff helps bring spiritual realities such as joy into our lives!

I find two reasons why many Christians aren't enjoying God's best—His joy, His direction, His peace. First, a whole mob of believers live "Christian" lives in their own pathetic flesh power. Spirit-control is essential. And second, though believers know they're supposed to obey and study and witness and fellowship and stuff, they still don't! If, under the Spirit's control, these factors are developed into habits of lifestyle, joy—and a whole bunch of other supernatural delights—*will* result. But the Spirit doesn't develop our joy on only an abstract, biblical level.

Hassles

The Holy Spirit makes sure we develop joy on a practical level through an unusual method. It's the knock-out-the-props method. And under Spirit control, it's guaranteed to bring joy.

"Just figure that it is complete joy, fellow Christians, when you fall into all kinds of hassles, when everything falls apart. You know the process, that the testing of your faith (Lord? Remember me? Do You realize what just happened?) results in strong endurance. Then that strength builds and builds, forming you into the person you always wanted to be. You'll be the best you can be, a whole, complete person, with nothing lacking in your maturity."

That's a Stearns paraphrase, if you hadn't guessed, of James 1:2-4. That passage presents one of the strangest processes in life—the process of maturity. It's a rough one. I always wish maturity would be something I could slip on like a velvet jump suit, that I'd grow quietly. And that's one of the benefits of God's rough program for maturity—it brings joy.

Think of it all in physical terms; then we'll overlay the spiritual process of maturity on our thinking. I run a mile every morning. Well, almost every morning. I run just to keep in shape, but I've got a wild and crazy friend who runs just to run. Like a quick 12 or 15 miles a day. Now when Crazy Dick started running, it was a hassle to him. It hurt. His muscles would moan aloud and his knees would squeak when he passed around the communion plates in church. But Dick knew that the exercise was good for him— he had faith that this was a good thing for him to do. And he knew that because of the hurts, his endurance would grow. In fact, the reason newly exercised muscles are so sore is that the muscle fibers actually tear a little; then as they heal back together they are stronger than before. It hurts physically to develop physically. Anyway, as Crazy Dick sensed this process working, he got really excited about his running. Soon, he knew, he'd be able to *really* run, to enjoy runner's euphoria, to accomplish something. He was happy about the pain he was going through because he knew what it would bring.

Here's how the method works on a spiritual level:

1. God allows you to get into a hassle. You end up with a problem that brings pressure, that hurts. Maybe it's a disease that makes you suffer physically, or your folks get divorced, or a friend you love hurts you, or whatever. I don't have to think up more problems for you, right?

2. The hassle tests your faith. It'll make you start wondering why God allowed this, whether He remembers you at all, whether He really loves you, whether He knows what He's doing. Now obviously the test of your faith isn't for God's benefit—He already knows how much you trust Him. The test is for *you* to decide to trust Him even in the middle of this mess. You don't understand it. You don't appreciate it. But you can still decide to trust Him.

3. Each test situation that you "pass"—by deciding to trust God in it—makes you tougher. And the tougher you get as a person the easier it will be to trust Him during your next hassle. You start seeing these situations as God sees them. You grow in spiritual maturity.

4. Your growth in maturity makes you a more complete person, more fulfilled. You enjoy the incredible treasure of becoming more and more the person you were meant to be. You're finding what you were designed for. Life makes sense; your wisdom is rich and deep. You're becoming more like the perfect Man—Jesus Christ.

5. And so, you can be excited about how God is shaping you through this hassle. Throughout the

process, in even "a great ordeal of affliction," you can have an "abundance of joy"! (2 Corinthians 8:2)

Hard to believe? Yup. Especially when you're in the middle of a hassle. But when you're finally coming up for air after the ordeal, you can look back and know that it was a valuable experience, that there was a good reason the Spirit could give you joy in such a miserable episode. The Bible suggests that after we've gone through the valley of weeping, we can look back and realize that our pain and our tears have made wells and refreshing pools (Psalm 30:5). There's a deep joy to be had in the hassles (see Acts 20:22-24).

Huh?

Did you get lost in the words back there and forget what we're doing? That we're looking for joy? Let's review the basics of it:

Joy is a spiritual state that comes from God.

Joy gives fantastic feelings even when pleasures don't make it.

God gives joy when spiritual control is a general characteristic of our lives.

In order to develop joy in us, the Spirit will direct us into biblical habits and practical hassles.

Now go ahead. You deserve it. Catch some joy!